Dedicated to
COLONEL ARTHUR L. CONGER, C.M.G.
as a token of appreciation for the work he is doing
in furthering the cause of Theosophy.

The author wishes to place on record his appreciation of, and gratitude for, the work his wife has done in typing the manuscript and generally helping in the preparation of this book for the press.

EVERYBODY'S GUIDE TO THEOSOPHY

EVERYBODY'S GUIDE TO THEOSOPHY

A simple explanation of the Theosophical teachings for the new student

by
HARRY BENJAMIN

"Give light and comfort to the toiling pilgrim, and seek out him who knows still less than thou; who in his wretched desolation sits starving for the bread of Wisdom and the bread that feeds the shadow, without a Teacher, hope or consolation, and—let him hear the Law."

H. P. BLAVATSKY (*The Voice of the Silence*)

THEOSOPHICAL UNIVERSITY PRESS
COVINA, CALIFORNIA

*Printed in Great Britain
at the Gainsborough Press, St. Albans,
by Fisher, Knight and Co. Ltd.*

CONTENTS

Chapter		Page
I	Introductory	13
II	What is Theosophy?	20
III	Reincarnation and Karma	36
IV	Man's Sevenfold Constitution	50
V	Life after Death	63
VI	The Hierarchical Structure of the Universe	74
VII	Creative Evolution and the Doctrine of Swabhâva	82
VIII	The Doctrine of Cycles; and Rounds and Races	96
IX	Man's Divine Destiny; Brotherhood a Basic Fact in Nature	109
X	Theosophy as a Way of Life as well as a Philosophy of Living; Pitfalls on the Path of Occultism	117

CHAPTER I

INTRODUCTORY

NEVER was there a time when the spiritual needs of man needed more assuagement than at present. Mankind is in the "melting pot" with a vengeance, and the vast majority of people seek blindly this way and that for help in extricating themselves from the cloud of doubt and negation that clothes their minds and souls.

Orthodox religion, the great corner-stone of faith of the past, has regrettably lost its sway over the minds and hearts of men. In these days of universal education, people are beginning to think for themselves, however rudimentarily in some respects, and so the creeds and dogmas that satisfied our forefathers seem sadly lacking in conviction and truth to-day. They carry a message at once outworn and ineffective to meet the needs of the times.

Materialistic Science that reared its head so proudly during the nineteenth century, when it thought that all the problems of the Universe were open to its investigation and solution, has since learnt to think again, and has discovered, much to its chagrin, that what it thought were no longer mysteries are still as great mysteries as heretofore, if not greater, in spite of the vast endeavours of scientists in all parts of the world.

Where matter was taken to be the "basic stuff" of the Universe, we now find the elusive electron, which, far from showing signs of materiality, seems more nearly akin to the shadowy elements of mind or spirit, formerly so ridiculed by scientific workers as having no possible shadow of basis in this solid and compact world. The further scientific investigation is pursued, the farther away seems to be the longed-for solution of Nature's problems.

Science and Industrialism have served well the material needs and comfort of mankind, it is true, in this twentieth-century world; but the inner, the more spiritual, needs have become increasingly neglected or lost sight of, the more the material side has been provided for successfully.

Modern thought has endeavoured to fill the gap left by orthodox religion and science, but present-day philosophy and psychology do nothing in the slightest to cater for the spiritual yearnings and searchings of present-day man, however much they may seem superficially to satisfy his intellectual cravings and curiosities. Deep down inside the consciousness of the vast majority of people is a feeling of despair and frustration, a feeling made even more keen and sharp because of the two world wars passed through.

The call from all the pulpits of the Christian world for a " return to religion " as a cure for the present " godlessness " of society, will never achieve its aim, even if the Churches were able to re-present the Christian faith in more modern guise ; that is, in a guise capable of meeting present-day needs and problems.

Christianity as a *way of life* has never been tried, because the original Christian teachings have long been lost under a covering of dogma and ritual, in which ritualism came to be regarded as the spirit of the Christian faith instead of the mere trappings. As no Christian church or sect, of the thousands in existence to-day, ever ventures to put forward any positive religious philosophy which *really* embodies the teachings and sayings of Christ, we can safely conclude that no matter how much there may be an attempt at house-cleaning within the ranks of the Christian " faithful," in order to grapple with to-day's evident fact of man's loss of faith in Christianity as a religion, the attempt will meet with no real success. Neither will any secular attempt at religious revival succeed, no matter how well-meant, if it is based on biblical Christianity, with its personal God, " salvation from sin," and similar dogma and shibboleths of orthodox Christian belief.

Men in the Western World want to-day a new attempt at meeting their spiritual needs and yearnings, based on an understanding of life's problems as lived in the twentieth century with its bewildering material progress but underlying spiritual barrenness. They want a philosophy of living that is both a *way of life* and at the same time a key to the solution of those seemingly insoluble problems arising out of the presence of those baffling antitheses of birth and death, happiness and misery, wealth and poverty, well-being and disease, that confront them day by day in a myriad conflicting, confusing and interacting situations and crises in their lives. Situations and crises which, by their constant appearance and unfortunate consequences, shake our faith in ourselves and make it impossible to believe in the existence of a beneficent Divinity of any kind.

That such things as war, pestilence, hunger, poverty and suffering should be allowed to exist in a world which they feel ought to reflect those qualities of justice, goodness and mercy they have been taught to regard as the essential attributes of Divine Power, outrages the ethico-religious sensibilities of honest-thinking and plain-speaking people all over the world.

It is that feeling—rather than the spread of Scientific Materialism—that is the chief cause of the breakaway from all orthodox religious beliefs that is referred to as " the godlessness of our age." It is not " godlessness," however; it is merely a sign of the despair (oft-times mingled with disgust) at the failure of orthodox religion to minister to the spiritual needs of the times felt by those who have learned to think for themselves.

Such people do not want Materialism, and the complete negation of religious belief of any kind that it implies; they want a spiritual and religious philosophy that *really* meets their needs in these vital departments of living, and which satisfies them *mentally* at the same time. *Such a new philosophy of living is right at hand, ready for all to have should they so desire it!* It is new simply because it is as old as time itself; for, being so hoary with age, it is dazzlingly new to modern man's gaze, when first confronted with it, as is so much else in the modern world, which befools itself with thinking it knows everything that has ever been thought or done in man's immense past.

Of course, such a belief is the merest absurdity, and is based on sheer intellectual conceit; for only by going back to the past and beginning again where in our living we went astray previously, can we possibly hope to go forward to that new era of happiness of mind and body, and contentment of soul and spirit, each of us is craving for deep down within himself. We repeat; it is only intellectual conceit that makes modern man look down his nose, as it were, at the past, and imagine he has nothing to learn from that source. If he is humble and contrite enough in spirit, the glory of the past can still help him to the satisfactory solution of the immense and seemingly insoluble problems of to-day, problems which orthodox religion, science and philosophy have alike failed signally to solve for him. And as we have just said, this light of the past is likewise seemingly something brilliantly and vividly new in its modern dress as put forward in the doctrines and teachings of what is known to-day as THEOSOPHY.

Theosophy is nothing new in itself; as just indicated, it is merely the wisdom of the ages given to present-day man in a form capable of meeting his needs of mind and spirit; in terms, that is, which are capable of reception and understanding by modern minds, permeated by the scientific and psychological and philosophical jargon of to-day. It is because there is an obvious and crying need for its teachings to be known as widely as possible at the present time, that the book the reader now has before him has been written. It is felt that no better contribution to the needs of the age could be forthcoming from one who has himself benefited more than words can describe from the doubt-dispelling rays of Theosophical illumination in the realms of mind and spirit. It is with the earnest hope that many more will benefit equally, both mentally and spiritually, that the writer has dedicated himself to his task.

Although the basic teachings of Theosophy are easily understandable by the average intelligent reader, it is no easy matter to keep from getting into mental deep-water when trying to explain all its ramifications, and its application to the problems of our age. Also, as Theosophy refers to the deepest secrets of cosmical construction and development, dealing with the births and deaths and future lives of Universes, no less than with the births and deaths and future lives of individual men and women (pointing the way—in the process—to wonderful vistas of splendour for the aspiring soul of man and thereby providing us with a message of hope for our destiny, that is at once inspiring, ennobling and sublime), it will be appreciated that it is no easy task to keep always to simple and easily understood language throughout a book such as this one. But that is the objective—to present to the reader as clear and simple an exposition of the Theosophical Philosophy as could be managed.

Again, we have also to bear in mind that what is easily understood by some people is difficult to grasp at first by others; so that the reader is urged not to become discouraged if he finds himself unable to appreciate fully the significance of this or that part of the Theosophical teachings at the first perusal. Let him read and re-read the present book a few times, if necessary, and allow what he has read to sink into his consciousness; gradually he will come to understand the inner significance of what he has been reading. It is this inner intuitive understanding that is most necessary if Theosophy is to be comprehended aright in the modern world; not the merely superficial brain-mind understanding that is sufficient for books on psychology, philosophy, or current thought generally. Theosophy appeals to the mind of man, first, but it appeals most to his *soul and spirit*; and until the mind is lit up from within by the flame of inner spiritual awakening, much that Theosophy can give to a soul-hungry world will go unrecognized for the spiritual sustenance it really is. *Spiritual manna, indeed!*

We trust, therefore, bearing the foregoing remarks in mind, the reader will approach the pages that follow in a spirit capable of extracting from their brief Theosophical teachings the germ of something that will act as the spark to kindle the flame of real inner awakening of the higher mental and spiritual potentialities lying dormant at present within so many persons in the Western World, because of lack of opportunity for their development in this modern era, with its accent on material progress and its neglect of the inner realms wherein the real life of man is to be found.

"*Man does not live by bread alone!*" How true, indeed! But few in this age have been able to find that nutriment for the soul and spirit that can lead to the growth of inner powers and potentialities which can bring man to a stature far beyond anything dreamed of to-day by everyday mankind. Man has a great destiny before him; a destiny so great, indeed, that to but know it transforms one into a different being by the mere appreciation of the fact.

But because of lack of knowledge of the spiritual-ethical

guidance that Theosophy can give, the vast majority of people in the Western World, feeling the uselessness of looking to orthodox religious sources for inspiration in affairs of the soul, are now turning to social, political and economic forces to bring about that inner transformation—that " change of heart "—they all feel to be so necessary to make them worthy inhabitants of the " New World " of the future they all instinctively look towards as the salvation from present-day sufferings. In other words, *inner change* has come to be confused with *outer progress* in the mind of modern man, and the one identified all too erroneously with the other.

Hence the tremendous interest of many persons in politico-social-economic experiments such as Socialism and Communism. These people have an idea that, in some mysterious way, such systems can minister just as effectively to their spiritual, as to their material needs. But man—whether as an individual, or as part of a social group or nation—can only change *at heart* by changing *himself* (from within) ; no changes imposed from sources outside himself in the economic, social and cultural fields can alter him intrinsically, although such factors can, of course, help to a certain extent to mould his nature *superficially*. It is only by *self-imposed effort*, effort directed towards the end of seeking to *know and understand oneself more and more*, and thereby striving to live a life that will lead to the unfoldment of the inner powers and attributes which link man to the " Gods," that *real inner change or progress* is possible to mankind. It is precisely here that Theosophy provides us with the greatest possible proof of its value. For, against the vast background of cosmic evolution it sketches for us (of which cosmic evolution that of mankind is merely one participating factor), it shows us the broad vista of man's past and future, as part of the evolving life of the spheres. It points the way towards the ultimate goal of human evolution: DIVINITY.

Within each of us is the divine spark lit by the flame from the *Central Source of All That Is*, and through an understanding of the Theosophical teachings, and their application in our lives, we can unfold steadily those capacities latent within us which can set our feet on the ladder that leads the soul, step by step, through the ages of recurring incarnation, to the level of Beings as superior to ourselves at our present level of development as we are to, say, the insect world. However mean and petty we may be here on Earth at the present moment, there is a future for man that is breath-taking in its wonder and glory, a future that "leads to the stars."

By showing the neophyte not only the "why and wherefore" of his existence, but also making clear to him the *path to the future* to be trodden as a fully-conscious co-operator with the *Great Cosmic Plan*, Theosophy can do immeasurably more for the seeker after inner enlightenment than any other Movement of our time. *It shows us the direction in which we have to travel to achieve our destiny, and also the steps whereby the journey can be accomplished successfully*. What else could do as much?

In case the reader may imagine the foregoing to be merely the idle vapourings of a mind intoxicated with a draught of crude but potent spirit, too heady for its weak powers of cerebration, we venture to ask that nothing should be pre-judged. *Let the teachings speak for themselves!* That is all for which we plead. With that plea we now desire the reader's patient company through the pages of this volume. We do not think he will regret the journey!

CHAPTER II

WHAT IS THEOSOPHY?

THE first question that will naturally arise in the mind of the reader is: "*What is Theosophy?*" Well, stated briefly, Theosophy (Greek, meaning God Wisdom, or Wisdom of the Gods) is the modern name given to the system of esoteric teaching, handed down from ages immemorial, which has formed the basis for all the great religions and philosophical systems of the past, Christianity included. It was the title chosen to designate the teachings brought to the Western World towards the end of the last century by Madame Helena P. Blavatsky (acting as the emissary of those custodians of the Ancient Wisdom who have kept jealous guard over it through the ages, safe from the defilement of the sacrilegious and profane), in an attempt to rekindle in Western Man the light of the spirit fast being dimmed by materialistic Science on the one hand, and orthodox Religion on the other.

Madame Blavatsky went to America and founded the Theosophical Society in New York, in 1875, and in spite of the grossest libels and calumnies hurled against her, was able to infuse gradually the thoughts and ideas connected with Theosophy into current world-thought to a greater and greater degree as the years passed, giving back a vital and spiritual basis for living to a world fast becoming the prey to materialistic Science through the work of Haeckel, Tyndall, Huxley and their associates, and the tearing down of the obsolete views and ideas of orthodox Religion which that work entailed.

At that time the controversy between Science and Religion over the Darwinian Evolutionary Theory and its implications was at its height, and it was taken for granted on all sides that one could never reconcile the two antagonists over the problems of life and death as they applied to Man. It was assumed that Science and Religion must necessarily and for ever be against each other; and Man had either to sacrifice his reason to his faith, or else sacrifice his faith to his reason.

WHAT IS THEOSOPHY?

There seemed no way out of the impasse until Madame Blavatsky came on the Western scene, and, with the aid of the teachings of Theosophy, showed that there need be no cleavage between Science and Religion if both are understood in their true light, and that, indeed, there is always true harmony between them *and Philosophy* if the facts of life and Nature are approached correctly.

Theosophy is essentially a synthesis of Philosophy, Science and Religion, but only in the sense of providing the basis for a correct interpretation of *all three* ; not a sort of hotch-potch of thoughts and ideas culled from this or that source, philosophical, religious or scientific ; but, we repeat, the basis from which all that is best and truest in Philosophy, Science and Religion springs. It was this priceless jewel that Madame Blavatsky brought to the Western World, and which has continued to leaven the thoughts and ideas of that world from 1875 onwards, in spite of the grossest misrepresentation and even ridicule. *Truth* will out, no matter how or where imprisoned ; and the truth that Theosophy brought to Western Man from that day in the year 1875, when the Theosophical Society first came to birth, cannot be shut out from the minds and hearts of those truly seeking for spiritual enlightenment.

In her two great works *Isis Unveiled* and *The Secret Doctrine* this great seeress left to posterity pearls of wisdom concerning the true nature of man, his origin, destiny, and relationship to the cosmos ; and the literature of Theosophy has swelled gradually to greater volume since those early days. At the death of the founder in 1891, at which time the Society had a membership which embraced the entire globe, the Theosophical leadership was entrusted to Mr. William Q. Judge and Mrs. Annie Besant. As these two could not see eye to eye on certain important points, the Society split into two main groups, one, under Judge, with its headquarters in America (now at Covina, in California) ; and the other, under Mrs. Besant, with its headquarters at Adyar, in India.

Later still The United Lodge of Theosophists was also formed (in Los Angeles), and The Blavatsky Association, in London, as well as other and smaller groups here and there ; so that there was quite a plethora of channels through which the original teachings of the founder of the Theosophical Society have found their way into the minds of the public. Naturally, when the founder of a movement dies, it is hard for certain minds to keep to the strict letter of his teachings, so that men and women have come and gone in some of the various Theosophical Societies and groups. They have sought to give *their own interpretation* of what Theosophical teachings *should* be, or *ought* to be, instead of confining themselves to the propagation of the actual Theosophical doctrines as first enunciated by Madame Blavatsky. This brought a certain amount of discredit in many instances upon the name of Theosophy itself in the process, through the misconceptions and wrongly-directed zeal of those responsible.

But *Theosophy* itself is, and must always remain, the *Wisdom of the Ages*. It is because the present writer feels that its least changed expression is nowadays to be found in the Covina Society, that he has given that Society his allegiance (although other Theosophical Societies are carrying on the Theosophical tradition as sincerely as they can and in a true endeavour to bring Theosophical enlightenment to the world). It is with the Theosophy of Madame Blavatsky that the present book is concerned and not mutilations or distortions of it.

We feel the reader should know of the various sects and groups within the Theosophical ranks, each with their own ideas as to what the main essentials of Theosophy are. In our desire to make Theosophy known to as large a body of people as possible, we wish to pass it on in an unchanged form (as far as our own understanding of the teachings will allow), and the Theosophical teaching emanating from Covina, in California, we regard personally as most akin to the original in spirit and outlook.

Let us begin, then, by trying to answer first of all the two most pertinent questions connected with our task:

(1) *How do we know the Theosophical teachings are what they are purported to be?* and,

(2) *Who were "they" who sent Madame Blavatsky into the Western World on her mission of enlightenment?*

Well, with regard to the first question, we can only say in reply that "by their fruits shall ye know them." By the inner understanding and wisdom they bring, these teachings stand

WHAT IS THEOSOPHY?

revealed to all earnest seekers after truth as pre-eminently the essential *Wisdom of the Ages*, that Wisdom taught in all the Temple Schools and Colleges of the Ancients, and in the "Mystery Schools" of Greek and Roman times, too. This body of Knowledge (of which Theosophy is the modern expression) has consistently formed the basis of all enlightened thought since Man could first think for himself, the teachings in question having been brought to him in the first place from planets more evolved than our own (in the evolutionary scale) by the custodians of that knowledge.

On our own Earth it has been jealously guarded by a line of Teachers (or Adepts) who still carry on the age-old tradition that has stretched backwards not for thousands of years but millions, into the vast antiquity of our Solar System. It is these "Adepts" who are the "they" queried above; and—in accordance with cyclic universal law, which ordains such periodic representations of the Ancient Truths in terms most suited to the age which needs them—it was as their Messenger that H. P. Blavatsky set out on her great mission to the Western World.

This inner knowledge *of the meaning and purpose of existence* is in the hidden keeping of these custodians of the Ancient Wisdom, and certain portions only are given out from time to time to humanity, through the medium of these periodic Messengers (of whom Madame Blavatsky was the latest), when the conditions make it necessary to try to save mankind from disaster—as at the present time—through the weight of ignorance, bigotry, and materialism which threaten to engulf it from all sides, not forgetting the gradually increasing craze for dabbling in psychic phenomena evinced in the West during the past century, a condition of affairs equally destructive to the best interests of civilized mankind.

H. P. Blavatsky, born in 1831, was the daughter of a Russian nobleman, and travelled widely in the East, searching deeply for occult understanding the while, and later was brought into direct relationship with the Teachers we have referred to, whose home is in the Himâlayan regions of Thibet. That such direct contact with the Adepts is an honour of the rarest kind, only those well versed in Theosophical understanding can appreciate; so that the spiritual worthiness of "H.P.B." for her great task stands revealed for all capable of real *inner* discernment to see for themselves; although she was not a paragon of all the virtues in certain exterior characteristics (a fact eagerly seized on by critics and enemies).

It is the destiny of all purveyors of new truths to be vilified and maligned by the very people to whom the truths are brought; so that it is not strange Madame Blavatsky met the same age-old fate. However, in spite of everything done to undermine her reputation in the eyes of the world, her message was heard eagerly by thousands of the most forward-looking men and women of the latter part of the last century. Theosophy has since spread itself steadily over an ever-increasing area of the world's surface, bringing new understanding and inner wisdom to all capable of grasping its archaic but epoch-making truths and principles. It has literally remade the world for many thousands, and will yet do so for hundreds of thousands more, as the knowledge of its teachings spreads ever wider afield.

It has been the custom for modern man to pride himself that the scientific discoveries of the past century are truly original, and earth-shattering in their effect on age-old religious and philosophical thought about the structure of the Universe, the origin of mankind etc. When, however, we begin to study Theosophy, we find, much to our surprise, perhaps, that the greatest discoveries of modern science, including Evolution, are nothing as compared to the knowledge of the inner construction and nature of the Universe which these teachings provide. It would, indeed, surprise our modern scientific enthusiast to know that Darwin's much-vaunted theory of Evolution was already known to ancient thought (not in its mutilated form as taught by Darwin and his successors, but in its truly enlightened form as one of the chief processes of Universal construction and development).

It has been referred to in ancient Brahmanical philosophical writings, as well as in the Chaldean, Egyptian, Persian, Buddhist, and even Jewish religious philosophies, to say nothing of the Greek and Roman. All the great religions of the past, in fact, whether connected with India, China, Persia, Egypt, Babylonia, Palestine, or elsewhere, had Evolution clearly defined as one of their basic tenets, although not always readily discernible to the exoteric eye; and the same with many of the still later "discoveries" of modern science, such as radioactivity, the vibrational basis of all matter, the relativity of Cosmic relationships (as outlined in Einstein's celebrated Theory), etc.

These teachings were hidden away beneath a coating of allegory, or in cryptic expressions to which the key was only vouchsafed to approved students, after proving their worth for such knowledge. What was put before the multitude was often only a mere fraction of the real knowledge possessed by those in charge of the religious and philosophical and scientific thought of their time. In short, the multitude was given the *exoteric* (i.e. outer or *merely superficial or external*) side of the teachings, in a form best suited to their understanding; while the *esoteric* (i.e. inner or *really spiritually illumined*) side was kept for those deemed worthy of such knowledge. So that if we now say the book of *Genesis* is an exoteric presentation of Cosmic truth, and not just the "fairy-tale" story it is assumed to be by modern thinkers and agnostics, and that its true understanding is to be found only in a study of those deeply esoteric writings of the Hebrews, known as the *Kabbalah,* it will perhaps not sound so strange to the reader as otherwise it might have done.

The same with the Gospels. When these are read in their esoteric sense, and not in the strict literal exoteric sense, it will be seen that Jesus propounded the same age-old truths as all the great religious teachers of world history before him, such as Krishna and Buddha of India, Lao-tse of China, Zoroaster of Persia, Orpheus of Greece, and the like. They all taught the *identical* esoteric truths, emanating from the same age-old basis of thought which modern Theosophy brings to the Western World; esoteric truths which orthodox religion has systematically misunderstood and misapplied, and which the modern scientific and philosophical world has pooh-poohed disdainfully as being mere "old wives' tales" and not fit for the serious consideration of "real thinkers."

While orthodox Religion persists in taking the bible allegories as *facts,* real events of the past, and while modern Science and Philosophy persist in regarding them as pure myths, with no relationship whatsoever to reality, so both sides will fail to grasp the essential underlying wisdom contained in these word-pictures of ancient truth about the nature and structure of the Cosmos and Man.

That is why modern man, falling between two stools as it were, finds himself without any real religious or philosophical convictions whatsoever, and heading more and more rapidly towards sheer materialism and spiritual bankruptcy.

It is therefore only *Theosophy* that can save civilized Mankind of to-day from its sorry plight, as neither present-day Science, Religion, nor Philosophy can get it out of the morass of negative thinking and doubt in which their dogma, creeds, and theories have landed it. Let us without further delay begin our study of these teachings, therefore, and thus make the way clear for the gradual enlightenment of the reader in those subjects of which he is most in need of inner understanding.

The Secret Doctrine, Madame Blavatsky's great work on the Theosophical teachings already referred to, gives *three fundamental propositions* which contain the basis of the *Ancient Wisdom*. These (analysed and explained simply later) are:

(*a*) An Omnipresent, Eternal, Boundless, and Immutable *principle* on which all speculation is impossible, since it transcends the power of human conception and could only be dwarfed by any human expression or similitude. It is beyond the range and reach of thought—in the words of Mandukya, "unthinkable and unspeakable."

. . . there is one absolute Reality which antecedes all manifested, conditioned, being. This Infinite and Eternal Cause . . . is the rootless root of "all that was, is, or ever shall be." It is of course devoid of all attributes and is essentially without any relation to manifested, finite Being. . . .

(*b*) The Eternity of the Universe *in toto* as a boundless plane; periodically "the playground of numberless Universes incessantly manifesting and disappearing," called "the manifesting stars," and the "sparks of Eternity." "The Eternity of the Pilgrim" is like a wink of the Eye of Self-Existence (Book of Dzyan). "The appearance and disappearance of Worlds is like a regular tidal ebb of flux and reflux."

(*c*) The fundamental identity of all Souls with the Universal Over-Soul, the latter being itself an aspect of the Unknown

Root; and the obligatory pilgrimage for every Soul—a spark of the former—through the Cycle of Incarnation (or "Necessity") in accordance with Cyclic and Karmic Law, during the whole term. In other words, no purely spiritual Buddhi (divine Soul) can have an independent (conscious) existence before the spark which issued from the pure Essence of the Universal Sixth principle—or the *Over-Soul*—has

(*a*) passed through every elemental form of the phenomenal world of that Manvantara, and

(*b*) acquired individuality, first by natural impulses, and then by self-induced and self-devised efforts (checked by its Karma), thus ascending through all the degrees of intelligence, from the lowest to the highest Manas, from mineral and plant, up to the holiest archangel (Dhyani-Buddha). The pivotal doctrine of the Esoteric philosophy admits no privileges or special gifts in man, save those won by his own Ego through personal effort and merit throughout a long series of metempsychoses and reincarnations.

No doubt the foregoing statements (embodying as they do a philosophical viewpoint of the greatest sublimity as well as the deepest profundity) may sound exceedingly involved and difficult of comprehension by the average reader, especially as some of the terms used are of Sanskrit origin (the language most identified with the Ancient Wisdom, as India was the real home of its presentation to the world of awakening consciousness which later developed into the early historical era).

Let us, therefore, attempt to translate forthwith the essence of the three propositions just enunciated into words more readily understandable by Western people.

What they tell us is: (1) At the root of the Universe lies THAT which is beyond thought and expression, which is yet the basis and cause of all universal life and form (all Spirit and Matter), because everything that manifests (whether spiritual or material) is part and parcel of its emanating essence. It is symbolized as THAT because our minds can form no adequate conception of It, and any attempts to give It a definite name or attribute would only limit It in our own consciousness. In short, It defies word or thought, being quite outside the range of human understanding. It is the CAUSE of all manifestation, but remains for ever unknown and unknowable.

(2) From this "Unknowable Essence" springs all consciousness, whether universal or individual, and each human soul is an integral part of that essence, having gradually evolved down the ages, through the lowest forms of manifested (and seeming non-sentient) life, up through higher and yet higher forms to its present condition of evolutionary development by incarnation in world after world of Cosmic formation (each such world, after a due period of activity, being followed by an equal period of repose or seeming extinction). It will go on developing until it reaches union with the *Basic Source of All*, from which it originally sprang as a divine unit of existence.

(3) That this evolution of the soul takes place over enormous stretches of time, through periodic incarnations followed each by a necessary period in worlds beyond the physical. Each such incarnation is essentially bound and regulated by the kind of life led in the previous incarnation (or incarnations) through the eternal law of CAUSE AND EFFECT. Effects follow previous causes from life to life and during each lifetime, until the soul is finally cleansed and purified from all dross (*through learning how to live in true harmony with the laws of its being*), and so can take its place again with its parent, the *Divine Source of All*. This is preparatory to beginning yet further evolutionary development in Spheres and Universes beyond all finite ken or understanding, as the great Cosmic Scheme moves inexorably onwards fulfilling its destined plan through Eternity.

(4) All souls emanate from the CENTRAL SOURCE OF ALL EXISTENCE (which is yet beyond existence *itself*), and return to that Source in due course, after fulfilling their pilgrimage through the worlds of Cosmic activity and repose, evolving through the various grades of life from pre-mineral, through mineral, plant and animal to the human. No soul, however great, gains any advantage for itself in any shape or form without having worked for it in previous existences (or incarnations). Those souls not making headway are held back solely by infringement of the laws of their being, through ignorance, selfishness, sensuality, etc.

All soul evolution is strictly in accordance, and through

co-operation, with *natural law,* as manifest in the Universe and Man.

(5) The factor which limits or aids development of each soul is what is known in Sanskrit as *Karma,* or simply the law of *cause and effect* to which we have already referred. It acts not from some source far outside the individual, but through his circumstances and environment, and his mental and physical attributes, allowing one person to develop the greatest qualities of genius, while inhibiting another and keeping him on the level of primitive thought and activity, in strict accordance with self-imposed effort, *or the absence* of it, exactly as the inner driving force (the same in all) is heeded or ignored.

(6) The self-same principle of incarnation, alternating with a period of rest (or repose) for recuperative purposes preparatory to beginning a further life-cycle, applies equally to all Universes or Cosmoi, as to the human being or individual soul (or any form of life whatsoever, for that matter). This cycle of birth and rebirth is an integral part of Cosmic manifestation of Spirit through Matter, through all Eternity, the process being one without beginning or end, as far as Man's consciousness can tell. The cycle is designed essentially to bring out all potentialities latent in the evolving consciousness of the entity concerned, whether Insect or Man or Cosmos.

(7) Everything emanates from THAT and eventually returns to that Divine Source, preparatory to yet further pilgrimages through Space in quest of ever-further expansion and development of consciousness. All life, no matter of what kind, is essentially an expression of this seeking for expansion of consciousness through ever-widening and deepening realms of existence; this seeking for ever-fuller and deeper consciousness of thought and feeling, on an ever-ascending scale of refinement, until reunion with the Divine Source of All is achieved, being the one and essential purpose of man's presence on this planet Earth.

That, stated as simply, lucidly, and briefly as we can, is what the esoteric philosophy, contained in the three fundamental propositions enunciated in *The Secret Doctrine* by Madame Blavatsky, sets out to tell us. The Theosophical doctrines which embody, amplify, and explain these sublime and profound occult truths concerning the origin and destiny of Man and the Universe, will each be dealt with in fuller detail in succeeding chapters of the present book. In the meantime, we hope the reader will read over carefully what we have just said in the foregoing pages —*several times if necessary*—to allow these truly great and noble teachings to seep into his consciousness and take up their habitat there. It will be the beginning of a new mode of thought and feeling epoch-making in its spiritualizing consequences within him, we can assure him.

Before going any further, however, the great fact we have to make clear to the reader, at this stage, is that the Theosophical teachings embodying the foregoing esoteric doctrines of the Ancient Wisdom are not just "ideas" to be kept in the mind, to turn over and compare with other philosophical or religious or scientific "ideas." They are the embodiment of a RELIGION OF LIFE OF THE DEEPEST PROFUNDITY AND MAJESTY, which demands, from those accepting it, *action* as well as adherence.

That is to say, we have to *live our Theosophy* as well as *accept* it, once we have made up our minds that the truths it expounds form the key to the unlocking of our understanding of the Universe and ourselves, which indeed they do. The living of the Theosophical life leads inevitably towards that purification and expansion of the individual consciousness which brings about eventual reunion with its Divine Source far more rapidly than could otherwise be possible. It is the true *Path of Ocultism*, the path all aspiring souls have to tread to reach the greatest and most exalted heights that Man can climb to in his pilgrimage through terrestrial existence, from life to life. It is not to be confused with those "Occult Practices" which have led many to judge Theosophy unfairly, as being a sort of forcing-house for the development of super-normal powers, such as astral vision, the exploration of Space from outside the physical body, etc. Such super-normal powers are often developed during the course of treading the Path of Occultism, *but are by no means to be confused therewith.*

The development of occult powers is not what Theosophy sets out to teach or give guidance on. Any seeking such an objective (to their great peril!) are advised to turn elsewhere for guidance.

It is Theosophy's main claim to recognition amongst discerning

WHAT IS THEOSOPHY?

men and women that it teaches us pre-eminently HOW TO LIVE in the most practical and sane fashion possible, in the everyday world, as well as providing us with a spiritual philosophy which is so profound and all-embracing as to render all others puny by comparison. The practical philosophy of everyday living it teaches its students makes them worthy citizens of the world, in every sense, as well as aspirants for the noblest destiny of Man.

In other words, Theosophy does not seek to make its adherents cranks or ascetics or bigots, or any of the other pseudo-spiritual misfits of present-day life we see around us, through the spiritual philosophy it teaches. Instead, Theosophy seeks to make men and women capable of playing their part in the practical affairs of the country in which they live, through the deepened understanding of all aspects of being it provides. The nature of those teachings is essentially *practical and common-sensical* as applied to everyday circumstances and situations, despite its innate spirituality, being only the unravelment and application of NATURAL LAW to the life of man *in all departments of such living,* whether individual, social, national or otherwise.

Theosophy is indeed *common sense par excellence* as it embodies the essential common sense of the Universe (i.e. the *Natural Laws* upon which all life and living is based); and that is the reason for its grim necessity in the world of to-day. Now, more than at any other time, Man needs a philosophy of living which can show him the true reasons for his present unhappiness, discontent, and lack of " spiritual grace."

Through the practical tuition it gives the student, Theosophy can lead him into a world new and shining wherein he can relive his life along entirely new lines, bringing with it not only the happiness he deemed irretrievably lost, but opening up a path of mental and spiritual development which literally " can lead him to the stars."

Man has been left helplessly saddled with the crumbling remains of religions which—through the effects of centuries of observance of dead-letter creeds and dogmas—have set up personal gods whose thoughts and actions are tinged by the self-same motives as those which actuate the human beings who are called upon to look up to them for guidance and sustenance, albeit thoughts and actions of infinitely larger range and power and efficacy than the human, and correspondingly all the more to be feared and placated. Theosophy, however, sets before us a picture of Divine Power and Consciousness, unsullied by the hand of Man, yet a picture which embraces all that is best and noblest and truly spiritual in all religions, no matter how degenerate they may have become in their exoteric rendering as a result of clinging to mere blind ritualism.

In short, Theosophy teaches us to *live our religion*, by showing us its true esoteric meaning, should we wish to remain Christians, Hindus, Buddhists, Moslems, Jews, Parsees, or whatever else. All religions have had Theosophy (*the Ancient Wisdom of the Ages*) as their original basis, at the time of their inception, as previously emphasized, no matter how misinterpreted or distorted the original teachings may have become since through sacerdotalism and priest-craft, or how stereotyped and orthodox their modern presentation.

In other words: the living spirit of all religions is one and the same, no matter how diverse their external characteristics, and *that living spirit springs from the same source as Theosophy*. No matter how dead and spiritless any religion may have become in its present-day rendering, it can be revivified with new spiritual life and meaning by its devotee understanding Theosophy and applying its teachings to the basic tenets of his faith.

Thus, Theosophy does not destroy religion, as many assert, although it shows the shortcomings of all current faiths; neither is it a special kind of religion of its own, as others have erroneously imagined. But by showing people what is lacking in present-day religion generally, and indicating how to make one's own religious beliefs really come to life and glow with true inner spiritual meaning, Theosophy is the greatest religio-spiritual force in the world to-day. Hence its tremendous and epoch-making value to those seeking spiritual advancement in a world bereft of spiritual enlightenment and guidance through the wranglings of orthodox religionists and scientists and materialists and agnostics and atheists, and all those others who seek to pin down the aspiring soul of Man by word or dead letter, and keep it away from the living truth which alone can set it free!

WHAT IS THEOSOPHY?

This, then, is the dynamic force of Theosophy, once one begins to understand its doctrines and apply them in one's own life. Before proceeding with the elaboration of its chief teachings in the succeeding pages, we should like to conclude the present chapter with a restatement of the objects and aims for which the Theosophical Society was first founded by that small band of workers, led by Madame Blavatsky, back in New York in the year 1875. These aims and objectives are:—

(1) To diffuse among men a knowledge of the laws inherent in the Universe.

(2) To promulgate the knowledge of the essential unity of all that is, and to demonstrate that this unity is fundamental in Nature.

(3) To form an active brotherhood among men.

(4) To study ancient and modern religion, science and philosophy.

(5) To investigate the powers innate in man.

Those, then, are the ends, towards the attainment of which the Theosophical Society was formed, and the one requisite for membership is acceptance of the belief in the *true brotherhood of man*, without distinction of race, class, sex, creed or colour. The reality of this brotherhood is indeed a living fact in Nature, as we soon begin to realize, once our eyes have begun to be opened by the study of Theosophy. It forms the one basic tenet to which all wishing to join the Society are called upon to subscribe. Apart from that, members may hold to any convictions or beliefs they wish, and remain within (or outside) the ranks of any religious organization or body they choose.

The Theosophical teachings are there for all to study, try to understand, and profit by, according to individual innate powers and capacity; but no one is forced to believe in them and subscribe to them *in toto* in order to become or remain an active member of the Society anywhere. There is complete freedom of conscience in this connection, and nothing has to be accepted as part of a definite creed or system of belief. That would simply make Theosophy only another of the all-too-numerous cults and sects of various kinds, extant to-day, with their insistence upon the acceptance of a definite and formal creed or set of tenets.

Such insistence means death to any genuine inspirational basis there may have been at the beginning to animate the system of belief in question. Where creeds and rituals and dogmas come along to blot out the living voice of the spirit, TRUTH can have no abiding existence. It is because the living voice of TRUTH plays forever through the Theosophical teachings we are now to outline in the following pages, that no attempt is made in binding potential members of the Theosophical Society to their rigid acceptance in any formal manner whatsoever. One accepts what one chooses out of what one can make of the teachings, and there is always room for growth and expansion of understanding and ideas as one cultivates one's inner intuitive powers during the course of one's studies.

No one, no matter how many years a student of Theosophy, can say " I know all there is to know about Theosophy." That would stamp him at once as an imposter and fraud. There is always room for growth and expansion in one's understanding and grasp of Theosophical ideas, simply because, as one grows inwardly as a result of one's studies of the teachings, more and more becomes apparent as the years pass. And so one goes on forever finding new light and inspiration from the teachings, and an ever-widening horizon of truth and understanding, fitting one to pass on the knowledge thus gained to an ever-growing circle of enquiring minds and souls.

Indeed, it is one of the prerequisites for the inner awakening and development of intuitive understanding and wisdom that one should pass on the knowledge one has gained from a study of the teachings to all those in search of the truth about the mysteries of life and beyond, and who seek such assistance. If one attempts to study Theosophy merely for *oneself,* i.e. for the mere satisfaction of adding to one's brain-mind store of knowledge, or even for purposes of pursuing one's *own* spiritual development without thought of others, then such study brings nothing of permanent value in its train, only disappointment and dissatisfaction with oneself and life generally. That is the inevitable working out of one of the *Universal Laws of Life* which Theosophy sets out to make clear to us in our studies of its doctrines.

And so—" to live to benefit mankind " being the first step on the path of occult development which Madame Blavatsky made possible to Western Man by her introduction of Theosophy to the Occidental World in the latter part of the past century—let us now begin on a more detailed study of its teachings in the light of Madame Blavatsky's sublimely altruistic utterance, which contains in itself the true essence of the Theosophical outlook on life, which the present book seeks to further in the best way it can.

CHAPTER III

REINCARNATION AND KARMA

WHEN thoughtful people look around and see the great amount of suffering and disease with which mankind is afflicted, it is not surprising that many of them assume that there cannot be a beneficent God in the Universe, or else " how could He permit such a state of affairs to continue?" they argue. It seems to them that if there *is* a God, he is either not concerned in the slightest with our trials and sufferings (and therefore all our prayers and supplications to Him for the alleviation of our plight are so many wasted words), or else He is powerless to undo the wrongs and injustices seemingly inflicted upon millions of innocent people who were brought into the world through no volition of their own, and have had no say whatever in the selection of the circumstances within which their lives had to be led.

Thus, to save themselves from this seemingly insoluble paradox, such honest and thoughtful people have thought it best to conclude that there can be no Ruler of this Universe in the sense understood by the religious systems of the Jews and Christians (which belief in an omnipotent and omnipresent God with infinite powers and capacities has saturated the minds and thoughts of the Western World for nearly 2,000 years).

They have, therefore, gone over to the side of Agnosticism, if not sheer Atheism, not being able to bring themselves to believe that religion of any kind can have any true validity after this seeming glaring contradiction.

Thus, the crude Occidental conception of a God, all-seeing and all-powerful, yet seemingly unable to care for His peoples as any Being of such attributes and magnitude ought to do (even when they serve him with humility and reverence in the way marked out for them by the religion which sets Him up before them as an object of worship), has tended to paralyse all honest thought about the meaning and purpose involved in the presence of pain, disease, and suffering in our midst, in those with minds really capable of thinking about such problems when not biased by orthodox religious beliefs and conceptions about the matter.

Such honest minds are powerless to extract any sense from the situation, simply because they have never been given an opportunity to study the truths inherent in the age-old doctrines of *Reincarnation* and *Karma*, which could set their minds free and at rest at last.

These doctrines are the common property of all Eastern peoples, having been embodied in their religious thought from its earliest beginnings, whether we consider Hinduism, Buddhism, Confucianism, Zoroastrianism, Mithraism, the ancient religions of Egypt and Chaldea, and even ancient Judaism (when lit by the light of the Kaballah).

These age-old teachings have also had their influence upon the religious beliefs of ancient Greece and Rome, as well as upon those of ancient Mexico and Peru and other countries and races. In short, the doctrines of *Reincarnation* and *Karma*, which it is our object to study in the present chapter, have been found embodied (more or less clearly) in *all* religions throughout man's history, with the one exception of present-day Christianity. Even then they were far from foreign to Christianity, until the Council of Constantinople (in the sixth century, A.D.), finally decided to expunge all reference to them from future Christian thought and teaching.

Thus was shut out from the Western World the only two doctrines which could make sense out of the sufferings and misfortunes of man, because they were prejudicial to a belief in the existence of an anthropomorphic God of orthodox Christian invention, which the Council of Constantinople wished to be retained at all costs, in medieval Christian thought, because it strengthened immeasurably the influence of the clergy acting as the intermediaries between such an anthropomorphic God and man.

An understanding of the doctrines of *Reincarnation* and *Karma* would inevitably lead people to realize that their sufferings and misfortunes are the result of their OWN misguided efforts in living, and that far from being on this Earth for the first time in their present life they have been in incarnation here time after time, sowing seeds of good or ill in one life to be reaped in other and future lives.

Orthodox Christianity, however, has tried to make its adherents believe that "sin" (and its attendant suffering) is something inherent in Man's nature, and can only be exorcised by a blind belief in and acceptance of Christian dogma, thus transmuting the unhappiness and misfortune of the present to a life of unsullied joy in a "Heaven" in a world beyond the grave.

So long as the vast majority of people in the Western World were unable to think for themselves, such views on the subject in question, as put forward by the Church, were naturally accepted without thought or comment, except here and there by an enlightened few, who mostly kept their thoughts to themselves for fear of persecution. Owing, however, to the spread of education during the past century, increasingly more men and women have come to realize the futility of such an attitude in the presence of the realities they have to face daily in their lives.

The inability of orthodox religion to explain away all the apparent contradictions of everyday living in terms understandable to and acceptable by the modern mind, has done more to undermine its prestige than any other single factor; and the priest or parson can find no possible way out of the difficulty. He is bound by his creeds and dogmas, and so is powerless to help those of enquiring mind, and with ability to think for themselves, in seeking to grapple successfully with the giant problem of the presence of disease, suffering, poverty and the other misfortunes of existence in a world which they feel ought to reflect the omnipotent goodness and divine mercy of its Maker (if such a Being should, indeed, exist).

It is only if we turn to the East and try to make ourselves acquainted with the ancient teachings of *Reincarnation* and *Karma*, common to all Eastern races and their religions, that we can begin to make any sense of the situation. For, from a study of these age-old doctrines, we begin to understand that by regarding the life we now live as the only one we have ever lived on Earth, and the only one we are ever going to live, we make it impossible for us to come in any degree to an intelligent appraisement of the problems of living that beset us daily.

If we were walking along a high road, for instance, and saw

traffic appearing and disappearing all the time out of the main stream, without being able to discover (through some optical delusion) that it had been coming and going from turnings or by-roads which led to and from the high road on either side, we would find it quite impossible to understand why this or that particular vehicle suddenly appeared to our view or as suddenly disappeared from it, out of the solid mass of vehicles in motion along the highway.

That is precisely the situation when we seek to view life without an understanding of the doctrines of *Reincarnation* and *Karma*. We try to make everything fit into this one life of " threescore years and ten," and because nothing seems to make sense when we do so, we conclude that there is no sense to be made out of the world because Religion and Science and Philosophy have nothing to offer us in the Western portion of the globe that can act as a key to the unlocking of our minds. We see people born blind or deaf or insane ; or people so poor that they have to live on the merest dregs of existence ; while others come into the world with every comfort and convenience of living at their command, and with every prospect of a happy and healthy future before them.

The apparent injustice of it all seems to us a sheer mockery of living. We feel that if there *is* a God, He is just laughing at us as we try to struggle along in a world so criminally designed that some get all the good things of life for no effort at all, while others have to put every ounce of energy into obtaining a bare existence for themselves (and those dependent on them), with every obstacle placed in the way of their advancement.

And we feel so disgusted with the spectacle that, in despair of the inability of anyone in authority in Church or State or Seat of Learning to show us the reason for it all in terms acceptable to the modern mind, we turn perchance to revolutionary methods of restoring "reason" and "sanity" to a mad world that no superhuman power seems able to help, or if existing, cares to help. Hence the turn to Socialism and Communism in the belief that such systems can restore meaning and purpose and dignity to life for the toiling and suffering masses of humanity.

In the fervour of over-enthusiasm it is forgotten that, by seeking to impose our own man-made ideas of justice upon the world as we see it, we may be actually upsetting *Divine Justice* in the process, because of our blindness to see it in operation through neglect of an understanding of doctrines of age-old existence, strange to the ears and minds of Western man. Socialism and Communism may seem to bring more of sanity and justice into life for many, but they equally would bring much evil and injustice to many others deprived of what they firmly believe to be their just rights and privileges. If " reason " is to be the arbiter, where are we going to set the limits of its jurisdiction over the lives of mankind? For even if we could even-out all the injustices of economic life, doing away with poverty in the midst of plenty, what about the " injustice " of chronic invalidism in some as compared with good health for others, or dullness of intellect for many as compared with mental genius for the favoured few of the human race? Not to mention all other inequalities of body, mind, and spirit which confront us on all sides!

What we have to realize is that however much we may attempt to redress apparent injustice (as measured by man-made standards) in the economic and social spheres, by legislation or bloody upheaval (and no one will deny the need for a radical change of outlook in these matters in many parts of the world), we are, as human beings, entirely powerless to remedy the apparent injustice of the vast ranges of difference in physique, mental ability, spiritual qualities, aesthetic appreciation and sensitivity, and the like, as displayed between man and man the world over.

The differences of body, mind, and soul are the things that make each individual man and woman quite unlike every other, which confer on them their essential " uniqueness " as human beings, and make them what they *really are*. Mankind, no matter how determined it may be in the future to run the world by means of " reason," is completely powerless to change this " uniqueness " of man as against his brother man. We have to *accept* and *build on* this divergence of qualities among men, not seek to suppress it, if we want the world to be a place worth living in! This is a point of vital importance nowadays, in view of the trend of current political thought, and the desire to make " all men equal."

We are all alike in many respects, no doubt, but in the things that count between individuals, we are, as just pointed out, totally different one from another. *There is still that uniqueness of self with which each of us is born to confound all attempts at equality.* We are born different from each other as regards physical, mental, and spiritual endowments in this life, because we have lived our lives in the past differently ; some doing harm to their physical, mental, and spiritual qualities by the manner of their living in previous incarnations, while others have cherished and nursed these qualities through their mode of conduct and behaviour. The end result of all this, for many earth-lives, is that some appear to come into their present life far better endowed and equipped for life's journey than their less fortunate brethren. Who is to blame? *Only ourselves.*

If the doctrines of *Reincarnation* and *Karma* tell us anything at all, it is that if we suffer in this world, we do so entirely because of our own previous mistakes in living. For the doctrine of *Reincarnation* teaches that we keep on returning to earth-life after a suitable period for rest and recuperation for the soul in higher worlds than the physical, where lessons from the preceding life are—or should be—taken account of by the reincarnating entity or ego until all the dross of the lower nature has been burnt off in the fires of suffering and tribulation during this recurring earthly pilgrimage of the developing soul of man.

It is through the operation of the law of *Karma* (which is simply the law of *cause and effect,* i.e. any disturbance of natural equilibrium produces an effect similar in intensity to the strength of its cause), that the *amount* and type of suffering to be endured in any particular earth-life is assessed in accordance with past mistakes and misdeeds.

In short: We suffer in order to grow in spiritual stature, and the degree and type of our suffering depend on the way we have conducted our lives in previous appearances on earth. What could be fairer? Is this not Divine Justice indeed? Our sorrows and sufferings are not, therefore, the outcome of arbitrary happenings or due to " ill-luck " or " Fate " ; we have no one but ourselves to blame for whatever befalls us, and no one but ourselves to assist us to get on our feet again, once down. We can call on " God," through supplication and prayer to help us, as much as we like, but if we are to overcome our difficulties, whether physical, mental, or spiritual, we have to look to *ourselves* for salvation, and no one else. That is the ruling Divine Law, and all the religions of antiquity have expounded this doctrine of personal acceptance of suffering.

It is because the Christian religion has made *salvation through Christ* its fundamental teaching that it has persistently led the Western World astray during the past two thousand years. People have been told that *Christ can save them* ; that their sins will be forgiven and that everything will be overlooked so long as they accept Christ as their Redeemer ; and it is only the very few who have made the discovery that it is *not* the historical Christ who can redeem them, as the Churches have taught, but the *Christ-Spirit* within themselves (their *Higher Self*).

It is the Christ-Spirit within man that can save him from the disasters in living brought upon himself by the actions of his personality (the lower unrefined nature) ; *that and that only.* Nothing outside himself at all. By making its devotees turn to a being outside themselves for salvation, the Christian Church has made it impossible for Western Man to find the true way out of his sufferings and mistakes in living.

To tell a man that what he has done wrong can be forgiven him by belief in an external " Saviour " is to mislead woefully. The Saviour lies within, and nowhere else, as just emphasized, and is a ray from the Divine Essence behind all creation. Until erring man finds out the truth of this statement, he must go on suffering, returning to this Earth repeatedly in different bodies until the lesson has been well and truly learned in the hard school of misery and distress.

The one purpose of suffering is to make us appreciate that we are living wrongly, and thereby forcing us to seek out our mistakes and rectify them. Once any particular mistake is rectified, suffering will cease in the direction or domain in question. But there will be suffering in other directions to contend with in life after life, until we have learned the *great lesson of all,* which is: *that we are sparks of Divinity, and that only by allying ourselves completely with the Divine Within* (the *Christ-Spirit,* if one likes to call it that ; or the *Higher Self* as we would prefer to name it) *and living according to Its behests, as opposed to those of the personality (or lower nature), can the way to final liberation and salvation be found.* Then only will suffering really begin to cease to plague our lives, and the way to true living be opened up for us at last.

As we achieve spiritual unity with the divinity within, through the gradual awakening and development of inner spiritual consciousness, suffering in the everyday sense as experienced by ordinary people will cease to have the prominent position it formerly occupied in our lives.

There will still be *spiritual* suffering, however, to endure for the aspiring soul until purified completely as it journeys up the ladder of life. For while there is life in the human body, suffering of one kind or another there must be; it is a law of our being; it points the way towards inner purification and salvation, as just emphasized. When we consciously understand this vital fact and its significance, we are in a position to act accordingly and do what is necessary to meet the contingency. Not like those who walk with eyes closed in the everyday world, enduring the kicks and blows of " Fate " without knowing the why and wherefore of their suffering.

Once our eyes are opened to the fact, not only are past mistakes in living adjusted through suffering, but opportunity is provided for further spiritual progress through the experiences passed through; each such experience being a door (as it were) through which the soul can pass on its way towards ever-fuller lifeknowledge and understanding. Thus the operations of *Karma* help our evolution all the time, while exacting payment for past infringements of Divine Law.

There is therefore no punishment, in the ordinary sense, in the happenings and circumstances of our lives, under the impact of *Karma,* as we journey from life to life in our pilgrimage through existence. Through the operation of the Divine Law we pay the price for our mistakes and misdeeds because no one but ourselves *can* pay that price, however much we may seek to put our burdens on other shoulders.

In paying the price, however, we are enabled to pass onward and upward in spiritual evolution, and we understand what is actually taking place. Could anything be more just than this, we ask? Of a truth has it been reported: *" Justice is mine, saith the Lord,"* for it is indeed Divine Justice that we see at work everywhere in the world around us, although superficially it may seem like the greatest injustice. What appears like justice to human minds is more often than not *injustice* according to the Divine Plan ; and what seems like injustice according to human standards is the working out of *the just laws of the Universe*.

So that, through an understanding of the ancient teachings of *Reincarnation* and *Karma*, as taught to the Western World through the medium of Theosophy, a completely new outlook on life and its happenings is obtained for the student. He no longer sees injustice everywhere, but Divine Justice at work in and through everything. But that is not to say that we have to sit still and see others suffer and just shrug our shoulders remarking " *It is their Karma.*" Not a bit of it. That is the way of the Pharisee. It is our duty to help our fellowmen, wherever and in what way we can.

The fact that we are united by spiritual bonds to all that lives should make us strive our utmost for such things as better living conditions for the down-trodden ; better methods of treatment for the sick and ailing ; better standards of education and vocational training for the masses ; and similar praiseworthy objectives. Such aims should be encouraged by all the legitimate means within our power. But let us not delude ourselves that by so doing we are bringing justice into an unjust world. That is the mistake of the Socialist and Communist, as already pointed out.

In all such things we are acting as but the unconscious agents of *Karma*; for *Karma* rewards us for good deeds as well as punishing us for bad. What we have always to bear in mind to temper any arrogance of spirit we may possess in these matters, is that *nothing man-made can undo the workings of Divine Law*. Therefore, if people have to suffer for past misdeeds until they have learnt the meaning of their suffering and " go and sin no more " (in that particular respect), they will have to learn their lesson in the manner most suitable, no matter how much their material environment has been altered for the better by enlightened social and political action.

We are, therefore, what we are at any moment of our existence, because of the action of the universal karmic principle in our lives ; the present being the outcome of aspirations and strivings of the past (or lack of them), while the future will develop out of what we are *now* doing with ourselves. " As we sow, so verily do we reap! " That is the basic principle underlying the operation of *Karma*, so that by enlightened action NOW (once we understand what is involved in the karmic process), we can plan our future by *positive day-to-day activity*, growing into *what we shall become* through the operation of the principle in question.

For *Karma* (even without our knowledge) aids our evolution by its curbs and checks, by pointing out (through suffering) our past and present errors (as already emphasized) ; so that when we now co-operate with its action *consciously*, it ceases to be our *mentor*, and becomes our willing *ally*, helping us to remake ourselves anew with its aid in the image of the Spirit, and fulfil our evolutionary destiny.

There is a great deal more that could be said about *Karma*, but we must leave it to the more advanced study of the student. One last thing, though : Our material circumstances and physical endowments do not necessarily reflect our spiritual status ; many are born in lowly positions who are very great souls indeed ; and material prosperity and comfort can be as great checks to spiritual development as their opposites. Everything depends upon the individual and his reaction to his circumstances.

Usually, when, by this time, people have begun to appreciate the reasonableness of the doctrines we are here discussing, they begin to ask questions. The first invariably is : " Why do we not remember our past lives if we have lived on Earth before? " This seems a very reasonable question to ask, but what such people fail to realize is that it is only the *Ego*—the higher part of man—which reincarnates, and not the lower self (physical body, emotions and lower mental qualities). These are put off successively at death and a new set put on at each rebirth, (as will be explained more clearly in a later chapter).

There is, therefore, no single factor remaining of the former physico-mental organism that can carry over the memory of previous incarnations. These memories are locked up in the Higher Self or Ego, *essentially*. Only as individual evolution reaches the higher levels of spiritual development can traces and memories of previous lives be unfolded to the vision of the lower being (i.e., when the lower bodies—or principles as they are called—are of refined enough texture to allow the necessary vibrations to percolate through to the lower consciousness).

Again, people will ask: "How do we *know* that life goes on after physical death in such a way as to make rebirth inevitable, and, indeed, part of the plan of Creative Evolution for the spirit of man, as you assert it does?" Well, the only alternatives to reincarnation are complete annihilation of every vestige of man at physical death, as materialist Science asserts; or Eternal Life in "Heaven" or "Hell" for the soul after the death of the body, as orthodox religion teaches.

Which of those three views seems the more logical and sensible? The view of materialist Science can be dismissed as being merely the outcome of ideas about life based on the conception that matter is everything and spirit non-existent. Yet, we now know that even matter is *immaterial* when analysed deeply enough, and leading physicists of to-day are putting *consciousness* as the ultimate basis of matter (i.e., Jeans, Eddington, etc.).

With regard to the orthodox view of life after death, in which one is rewarded or punished for what one may do in the present life (no matter what the circumstances of birth and physical, mental, and spiritual endowment may have been) in an *eternity of either joy or torment,* this is such a pathetically weak conception that very few Christians really believe in its truth. It is so palpably unfair and unjust. Besides, why should souls specially created at each fresh birth become eternal thereafter? Eternity embraces the past as well as the future, and the Theosophical conception of eternal life is therefore far more logical than the Christian, in every way. To be allowed to come back time after time, in suitable environmental conditions, and with physical, mental, and spiritual qualities which we have earned, to try once again to make a better job of things than we accomplished last time, is surely by far the more sane idea, and far more in keeping with real Divine Justice.

But people always say: "Yes, but what *proof* have you of all this?" Well, to that question we pose another: "What proof have *you* that your particular view is correct?" *None whatever.* So why put all the onus of proof on us? The materialist has no way whatever of proving that his contention is the true one, neither has the orthodox religionist. Whereas the Theosophical conception throws a wonderfully revealing light on the reason for man's travail and suffering, and accounts for all the countless differences and divergencies at birth between people, physical, mental, and spiritual ; how does either the materialistic or orthodox religious view bear on these subjects? *Neither can explain anything !* Both give a point of view that does not in the least fit in with the facts of life as lived in the world we see around us. Only the Theosophical viewpoint makes things intelligible, at last, because being based on the Eastern acceptance of the age-old doctrines of *Rebirth* and *Karma.*

There can therefore be no objective proof—in the physical sense—of the truth of the doctrines we are discussing in the present chapter ; their validity lies essentially in the fact that they explain life and its problems so very much better than any other approaches to the subject. In the East, there is no difficulty in accepting the idea of returning repeatedly to earth-life, in new bodies ; it just seems strange to Western minds, because unusual, that is all. Once the idea is allowed to sink in, and is not mixed up with notions that people sometimes come back to animal bodies, and similar crude misconceptions, it grows increasingly obvious that rebirth is an essential feature of life and part of the *cycle of existence.*

Life is essentially cyclic in character, as witness the wheeling planets in the heavens ; the progression of the seasons, each in turn through the year ; the following of day by night, to be followed again by day ; the shedding of their leaves each year by the deciduous trees, followed each spring by a fresh outputting of new leaf ; and so on and so forth.

Everything in Nature is cyclic, if we study the matter carefully, and rebirth is only one expression of this fundamental principle. Where people go wrong is in assuming that the Mr. Smith or Mrs. Jones they are now will be reincarnating again in the next earth-life ; whereas this is quite untrue. The Mr. Smith and Mrs. Jones of the present are only the outward expression of the Ego which inhabits the body, emotions and mind of these entities. It is the Ego (or Higher Self) which brings about the reincarnating each time, in a new physico-mental-emotional garb to suit the needs of the new life, but made up of material which owes its origin directly to the way in which the former physical, emotional and mental framework of being was used or misused previously. (This we shall explain more fully in a later chapter dealing with the *Seven Principles of Man*.)

Again, there is a great deal of confusion of thought about the time between incarnations. The periods between births can vary very greatly as between individuals, depending upon the degree of inner development of the entity concerned. For instance, the savage would probably reincarnate very soon after death, because he would not have much that is of value to the growing soul in the experiences of his past life to work into that soul's qualities preparatory to its next visit to Earth for fresh experience towards future development. Whereas, a highly-developed individual might spend thousands of years in the after-death state before returning to earth-life again, imbibing the experiences of the former life into that higher spiritual part of his being, to be worked on and over until made into qualities and characteristics that will help on the further evolution of the self in its successive earthly pilgrimages. We must leave further study of this part of the doctrine of *Reincarnation* to the student's deeper penetration of the Theosophical Philosophy.

In a book like the present we can only touch lightly on the various aspects of the subject, and, we hope, having whetted the reader's appetite for more, leave it to him to go forward with the study of the more recondite Theosophical writings.

To recapitulate, before bringing the present chapter to a close, it may be said that part of us *which we feel and know* is only the *outward expression* of an entity which is gradually evolving through the ages, in successive earth-lives, interspersed with periods for rest and recuperation, and for absorption of material derived from earth experience which will be of value to the evolving Ego in realms beyond the physical. The conditions of each birth and the life to be lived in each incarnation are controlled and directed by the principle of *Karma* (which is always in action in the Universe) rewarding for good deeds and aspirations and penalizing us for wrong-doing of all kinds in order to make us increasingly aware of the fact—as we travel through life after life—that we are here not for our own benefit or pleasure but to fulfil a destiny already marked out for us by THAT WHICH

SENT US INTO THE UNIVERSE, and to which we shall return when our pilgrimage has been successfully completed.

When the spark of Divinity that is the central core of each of us has had its attendant principles sufficiently purified through countless earth-lives, and (with the yield of experiences gained during those earth-lives in its keeping) has at last attained a degree of self-consciousness which takes it beyond the scope of our Earth-Sphere, there will then be no need for further rebirth in the physical world. *Karma* will have worked itself out at last and have lost all its force in that particular instance. For what was once an unselfconscious god-spark will have become " one with its Father in Heaven," so to speak. It will enter a realm of glory and future development of spirit that is quite outside our ken.

But there are some who turn back from this final liberation of the spirit, in worlds beyond, to help on their fellow-men in their onward and upward struggle, and these are the beings who dedicate themselves to forwarding the evolution of humanity through the ages as helpers and guides. The Great Beings who watch over the destiny of our globe are of this august body, and those we call " The Masters of Wisdom " are the links between them and us. These " Masters " have achieved full self-consciousness as far as mortal man is concerned ; but before passing on to higher worlds of being and further glories, they have dedicated themselves to helping us on the upward path of spiritual enlightenment. We shall each of us, in due time, become like unto them in wisdom and spiritual stature ; that is part of our evolutionary destiny ; just as it is our further destiny still to become gods in our own right when the divinity within has been allowed to blossom fully. But we are here talking of the very dim and distant future, indeed! For the present, let us be content to learn the lesson that an understanding of the doctrines of *Reincarnation* and *Karma* can teach us and apply our knowledge here and now in furthering in the present life our inner development and that of our fellow-men. That will be enough for a start!

CHAPTER IV

MAN'S SEVENFOLD CONSTITUTION

ACCORDING to St. Paul, man is a trinity composed of body, soul and spirit. As far as it goes, this is a very good way of splitting up the entity Man into his component parts; far better than the "scientific" view that man is just a mind and body, which is the current psychological conception. There are many grades of present-day psychological opinion; ranging from pure materialism—where man is conceived as being just a body and brain, with the mind as a sort of excrescence of brain-functioning (everything purely material and physical)—to those psychologists who conceive man as being more mind than body, with the mind controlling and directing everything through the medium of the brain and nervous system.

In recent years the idea that the mind has various layers has come very much to the fore, through the work of Freud and his disciples; but Psycho-Analysis (the system of mental therapeutics Freud originated), has come into rather ill-favour in many quarters, because of its undue emphasis on sex as the mainspring of everything in the mental and emotional life of the individual. No one would deny that psycho-analysis has done good work in making known to modern man the hidden workings of his subconscious levels of being, but Freud's views have been made, as it were, into a sort of religion by his followers, and a very ugly twist has been given thereby to the human psyche by those holding and accepting that viewpoint.

A refreshing advance on this attitude is to be found in the work of two former disciples of Freud—Adler and Jung, and the latter approximates very closely in his later work towards the outlook on life that the Eastern Philosophers and Psychologists have adopted for thousands of years. To us Westerners, so accustomed to regard everything that comes from the West as far superior to that from the East, it may be rather a shock to learn that, in the realms of deeper thought generally the East is far more advanced in every way than we are, as witness the Theosophical Philosophy we are now studying.

In the realm of psychology the East is far and away ahead of the West in its understanding of the human *being* and the working of his component parts. From time immemorial the Eastern teacher has split up man into seven bodies or principles, in order to explain to his disciples what man is, and how we can best understand and study the workings of his inner components. This sevenfold constitution of man is the one followed by the Theosophical student in his studies. It makes everything very simple when trying to understand what it is that dies ; what it is that lives on after the death of the physical body ; what it is that reincarnates ; and what it is that lies at the central core of all : at the heart of man's being.

The best way we can introduce the reader to the subject is to think of the spark of Divinity already spoken about as being the central factor in man, as being the inner principle of all, the highest of the seven. This, then, clothes itself in another principle, the sixth, in order to gain expression in lower worlds than its own ; then in the fifth principle ; then the fourth ; and so on until the full seven principles are there, with the spark of Divinity at the core of all, and working and radiating through them. Its effect on the lower and more dense principles (or bodies as they are called) is very weak, of course. Its influence and impulses are felt even only dimly by some of the higher bodies ; but it is the mainspring of all, and is that which links each living being to every other ; for we are all sparks of the same Divinity and therefore all of the same spiritual basis and origin.

Before the various principles or bodies can be intelligently visualized in his mind by the reader, it is necessary to make it clear that, in the Theosophical teaching, it is expressly understood that there are varying grades of matter in the Universe, ranging from the densely material (the matter of our physical world) through ever-finer grades of matter until the finest and rarest of all is reached, wherein man's highest principle resides. People have accustomed themselves to regard matter as all alike, and all the same as the matter of our physical globe, from which our physical bodies are also manufactured.

But Science to-day has shown us that the electron—which is

the basic unit of physical matter—is not even material in the commonly-accepted sense (it is merely a charge of electricity). Scientists are beginning to perceive—albeit only dimly perhaps at present—that there may be shades and refinements of matter which entirely elude our physical grasp, even with the aid of the finest instruments. The "Ether" has been regarded vaguely by scientists for a long time as a sort of cradle of all manifestation of physical phenomena. But, to the Theosophist (and those ancient philosophers who have been the source of Theosophical inspiration), the scientific "ether," so ambiguous and illusory, is only the shadow of the real *Cosmic Ether* which is the germinating ground for all that has material existence in the Universe, ranging from the very finest and rarest forms of matter down to the most densely physical. It is the plenum and source of all, and all matter reverts to it from time to time for fresh working-over and renewal, as part of the vast, unending cosmic process of life, decay, and rebirth to new forms.

In the Theosophical view everything connected with our world is "septenary" in character; by which is meant that everything is graded in series of sevens, seven being the *keynote* of our sphere. Thus we have the seven prismatic colours; the seven notes of the musical scale; and so on. And matter, too, is divided into seven ranges (or planes) of density, these planes rising in series from the purely physical—the densest of all—to the rarest, which is the seat of all that is highest in our scale of spiritual evolution.

These seven planes of matter, avoiding the use of Sanskrit terms which are apt to be rather confusing to the beginner, and starting with the highest (or 7th.) can be designated: *The Divine; The Spiritual; The Intuitional; The Mental; The Emotional; The Etheric;* and *The Physical*. Every human being has a body constructed from each of these various grades of matter (welded into one whole, as it were), the seventh (or highest) being so rarified as to be practically pure spirit, and the first (or lowest) being the very coarsest form of matter of all (the dense physical). It must not be assumed, however, that in this sevenfold division of matter we have one plane or layer piled up on the next lower, each plane divided by a sort of line from that below or above. Far from it. What we have to think of is rather an *interpenetration*

MAN'S SEVENFOLD CONSTITUTION

of the lower by the plane next above, on up to the highest of all, so that the matter of the seventh plane penetrates all other layers of matter below ; that of the sixth plane all below it ; and so on down to the lowest, the physical, which of course does not penetrate anything itself but is penetrated through and through by all higher categories of matter.

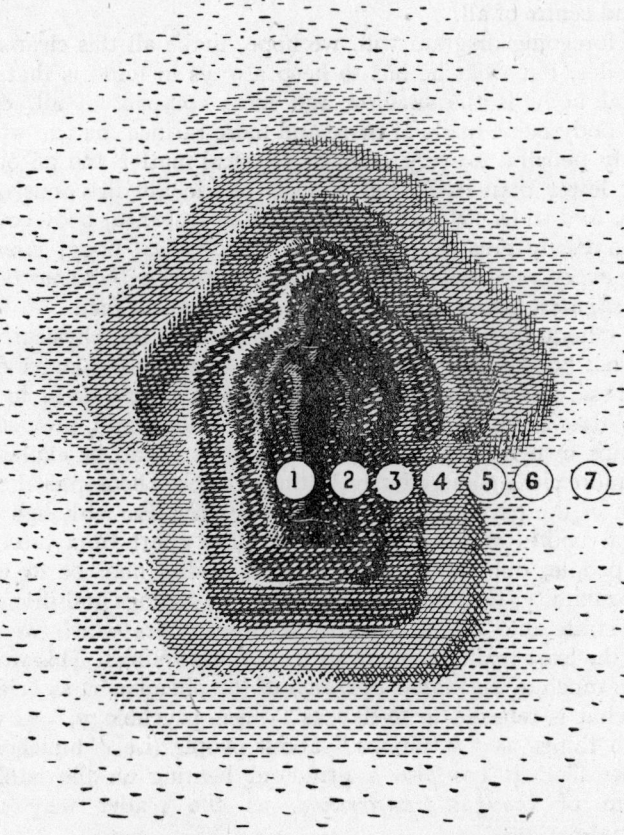

1. Physical Body
2. Etheric Body
3. Emotional Body
4. Mental Body
5. Intuitional Body
6. Spiritual Body
7. Divine Body

Thus we can visualize man, according to the Theosophical conception, being composed of the physical body (the densest matter of all), penetrated through and through by the etheric body (the next highest); then these two bodies by the emotional body (the next highest); then all these three bodies by the mental body (the next highest); and so on up to the seventh or highest body, which interpenetrates all other bodies and is the core and centre of all.

The foregoing diagram will, we hope, make all this clearer to the reader, but what he has to keep always in mind is that the physical body is the smallest and most compact of all, each higher body being made of more and more rarified matter, which not only penetrates every atom of physical matter and all other matter lower than itself, but spreads out in all directions over a wider and wider field, so that the highest (seventh) body covers an area vastly greater than that of the physical body, *directly linking every unit of humanity with every other, without our being in the slightest aware of this profoundly important fact.*

The etheric body occupies a larger field than the physical, the emotional body a larger field still, the mental body a larger field than these, and so on; so that perhaps it may now occur to the reader that many things he could not understand previously about his own feelings, thoughts, and actions can be explained much more clearly and effectively through this Theosophical conception of the psychological make-up of man. For although our physical bodies may on occasion be quite apart from those of other people, our emotional or mental bodies may be in very close proximity, thus making it possible for feelings and thoughts to penetrate into our consciousness from others which we did not in the least realize came to us from those sources. This would explain much of the *modus operandi* of the phenomena associated with what is referred to to-day as "mass psychology," as well as such things as "intuitions" about people (i.e. "hunches") and the like. It has also a profound bearing on the baffling problem of *thought transference,* as the reader may now appreciate.

Of course, there is the *real intuitional body*, higher still than the mental, and still more widely diffused, therefore, through which we may sometimes contact the thoughts and inspirations

MAN'S SEVENFOLD CONSTITUTION

coming from those "Higher Beings" than ourselves who have the evolutionary destiny of the human race in their keeping. This explains much of what is called "creative thought" or "creative inspiration."

Thus, through an understanding of what the idea of the seven principles entails, our appreciation and conception of man and his inner workings are made profoundly clearer and more understandable in every way. What a contrast to the psychology of the West, so glibly taught in our schools and universities! In contradistinction to the wonderful understanding of the inner workings of man that Eastern psychology provides, the psychology of the West can be regarded as touching merely the very outward fringe of the matter. The more that Western psychologists will humble their pride and look to the East, therefore, the more understanding of their subject will they derive, as quite a number of the best brains in the Western world are beginning to realize.

Having thus, at least superficially, made the reader somewhat acquainted with the (to Western minds) mystery of the inner psychology of man, we can now go ahead with the more interesting aspects of this most fascinating of subjects. Through an understanding of the seven principles we can at last begin to appreciate exactly what it is that dies at physical death; what carries on after that most potent of events; what it is that reincarnates in a new body later; and what it is that eventually becomes "One with Its Father in Heaven" and achieves man's crowning destiny: *that of Godhead* at the end of the climb up the evolutionary ladder.

The three highest principles, namely the seventh, sixth, and fifth are all usually linked together in Theosophical terminology as the *Ego (or Higher Self)*; that is, the divine body interpenetrating the spiritual body, and the divine and spiritual bodies in turn interpenetrating the intuitional body, unitedly comprising the *Ego* or highest part of man. *It is this Ego which reincarnates from life to life.*

The four lower bodies are used as vestures by the reincarnating Ego and are divested each in turn at or after physical death, and fresh lower bodies are taken on (donned as it were) by the Ego as it re-descends into the lower realms of matter at each fresh incarnation. We shall be dealing with the after-death state in our next chapter, and so we do not wish to say too much about it at present. Once, however, the reader grasps the fact that it is the Ego which is the reincarnating entity, and that the four lower bodies are not included in the scheme of reincarnation, he will begin to understand much that before was extremely puzzling, to say the least.

During each earth existence (or incarnation) the Ego undergoes experiences it could not otherwise have experienced *consciously*, because they are foreign to its *own plane of being*. It is necessary for the Ego to descend into the lower planes of matter, therefore in order to become increasingly self-conscious *on those planes*, transmuting latent potentiality for self-expression in these lower spheres into actuality.

When complete self-expression on all planes below its own has been realized by the Ego, no further point would be served in its reincarnating again into the lower realms, and therefore the Ego would cease to have thereafter any connection with these worlds of matter. It would remove itself altogether out of the ken of the lower planes, and concern itself exclusively with functioning in the highest material realms known to it, so as to achieve self-conscious experience and expression of an ever more spiritual nature and quality *which it could not otherwise have experienced, however, without the preliminary periodic sojourn in the planes lower than its own*. In other words, its consciousness would not have been developed sufficiently to make the experiences on these higher planes possible.

The reader will therefore understand that it is only by incarnating (in bodies suitable to those spheres of matter) in the mental, emotional, etheric and physical planes that the Ego can learn the lessons appropriate to those worlds of material existence. The essence of the experiences passed through in those spheres in each life are imbibed by the Ego in the after-death state, to be built into itself as qualities and characteristics to be used increasingly more completely in future earth-lives, until every potentiality and aspect of creative quality has been explored and worked-over in the thrust for creative self-development of the ever-onward-urging Divinity within.

It is this essential Inner Divinity which, clothed in the bodies of the matter of the spiritual and intuitional planes, as well as of its own to form the Ego (as just explained), is for ever striving to fulfil its destiny as an atom or particle of that *Central Divinity* which is the source of all creation in the Universe. To do this effectively it must experience life fully *on all planes,* from the seventh (its own highest) to the first (the lowest and densely physical), as already briefly indicated. This atom or particle of Divinity begins as an *unselfconscious God-spark,* an offshoot from its parent, *the Divine Source of All.*

As the Ego (clothed in the bodies it possesses on its own and the spiritual and intuitional planes) passes through countless reincarnations it slowly becomes increasingly conscious of its powers, potentialities, and attributes, thus eventually becoming that "Son of its Father" it is destined to become, through gradually evolving spiritual awareness of itself in contradistinction to (and as part of) the surrounding Universe. It fumbles and stumbles along, at first, clothed in the body of a savage, gradually becoming more and more civilized through succeeding bodies, learning its lessons in the hard school of misery and suffering, with fleeting joys and pleasures to make life bearable. Until, controlled and limited by its *Karma,* it emerges slowly into increasing consciousness of its destiny and begins to visualize itself for what it really is—a self-evolving particle of Divinity—thereafter allying itself *consciously* with its *Divine Purpose,* instead of evolving blindly onward as before.

From then on *the Ego directs consciously its own evolutionary development increasingly more as each incarnation is passed through,* until it reaches the stage of *fully self-directed evolution*—the stage which the "Masters of Wisdom" (already referred to) have achieved, which means development in full conscious accord and union with the *Divine Plan.* This point in evolutionary progress reached, the need for further incarnating in the lower realms of matter will become progressively less and less necessary for the Ego (as already briefly explained). It will have learned its lessons in living and be ready to pass onward and upwards, to worlds entirely out of human ken.

That is the destiny of the Ego, and it depends upon the kind of earth-life led in each incarnation as to the time to be spent in each after-death state by the reincarnating Egoic Entity (this being one of the topics to be dealt with in more detail in the next chapter). The qualities and characteristics strengthened and developed in each earth-life are built into the Ego's consciousness, to be made use of more completely in succeeding earth-lives, as already made clear.

In a book such as the present it is not possible to go very deeply into the various aspects of the Theosophical philosophy. It must be left to the reader to turn to the more recondite Theosophical literature for a deeper study of the teachings, once his appetite has been awakened by the mere sketch of the vast sweep and profundity of the subject which comprises the present volume. But many points not dealt with in fuller detail in the present and previous chapters will come up for attention more than once in later chapters, and the reader should not feel too upset if much of what has been said hitherto seems beyond adequate comprehension. It is the same with us all when we first begin to study Theosophy or any other " deep " subject.

It takes years of concentrated effort to gain a really full understanding of the main Theosophical teachings ; so that for the time being the best thing for the reader to do is to concentrate merely on obtaining a grasp of the general picture we are here trying to paint for him, and leave the details to be filled in later. Continuing, therefore, with our brief sketch of the sevenfold constitution of man, it is worth noting that every plane of matter is vibrating at a rate seven times more rapid than the plane below. We most of us know nowadays that everything in the Universe is in a state of vibration of its particles. If the rate of vibration of physical matter is taken as seven units, then etheric matter will have a vibration of 7^2 units, emotional matter of 7^3, and so on. Each higher plane has a material basis, very much finer and more rapidly vibratory than the plane below, so that etheric material is very much more subtle than physical matter, emotional matter much more tenuous and rapidly vibratory than the matter of the etheric plane, mental matter very much more rapid in vibration and response to stimuli than emotional matter, and so on.

The reader may be confused considerably by our reference to etheric matter, emotional matter, mental matter, and so forth ; but if he bears in mind that we each have bodies of matter of those planes, in order to be able to function on them, he will begin to appreciate gradually the great value of such an approach to the subject. For instance, in present-day psychological literature, feelings and thoughts are spoken about without any idea where they exist in relation to ourselves who have the feelings and thoughts in question. It is taken for granted that we *have* thoughts and feelings, because we are all conscious of experiencing them; but *where* they are experienced no one quite knows. They are assumed vaguely to be the result of, or associated with, what is termed *mental* activity, but where such activity actually takes place no one seems to know, either (except that it is somewhere inside ourselves).

When, therefore, in accordance with the Theosophical philosophy, we begin to think of the various bodies or principles, we at once appreciate that emotions (or feelings) are felt in the emotional body which interpenetrates the denser etheric and physical bodies. Thoughts are experienced in the mental body which interpenetrates the denser emotional, etheric and physical bodies.

Our emotions and thoughts have a life of their own, in their appropriate bodies, and can be seen by those with clairvoyant vision. They have a form and colour in accordance with their nature and quality, and there is quite a literature about the subject for those who care to delve more deeply into the matter. It has its fascination and its pitfalls, as all else in the occult realm.

The fact that feelings and thoughts are things with a life of their own (their life being in direct relationship to their intensity), will probably come as a surprise to many readers; but once we realize this fundamentally important fact, we will begin to appreciate the vital need for control over our thoughts and emotions. For if *uncontrolled* they can dominate us (as well as others), as many have found to their cost! They are disseminated into the mental and emotional worlds of matter, and are attracted to those susceptible to such attraction by suitable affinity of thought and feeling.

The more positive and dynamic our thoughts and feelings, the more they act for our benefit, because the matter they are composed of becomes more vibrant and effective as a direct consequence. The more negative and static our thoughts and feelings, the less they react for our advantage, and the more for our disadvantage, becoming just so much dead-weight on the composite being we are. Thus there is a whole world of philosophy locked up in this understanding that thoughts and feelings *are things* and can act for our good or ill (and that of others) according to how used by us (whether wittingly or unwittingly).

The etheric body is the body closest to the physical, and it is through the etheric body that the vital force of the Universe enters the physical body and gives us our vital power or energy. Energy does not come from food as modern scientists tell us ; that is an entirely wrong conception. Food is necessary for the effective utilization of energy, just as an electric wire is necessary before an electric current can function effectively ; but food does not create energy any more than the electric wire creates the electric current. The wire merely acts as a conveyor ; and precisely so does food.

We have dealt with the question of the relationship between food and energy in some of our other books and writings. Once, however, the reader realizes that his vital energy does not come to him through food, and is poured into him directly via the etheric body from the vital fount of the Cosmos (in accordance with his Karmic destiny, physical attributes, manner of life, etc.), he will have made yet another important step onward in his quest for that true wisdom which the study of Theosophy will help him to achieve. It is the etheric body which acts as the link between the mental and emotional bodies on the one hand, and the physical body on the other, bringing about that closeness of union between thought and feeling and action of which we are all so acutely aware. At physical death it is the physical and etheric bodies which disintegrate, leaving the emotional and mental bodies quite intact to carry out their duly appointed tasks in the after-death state, to be described in the next chapter.

The intuitional body is the body which is the home of the Ego, in our present stage of evolution, and from it all creative thought and inspiration flows into us. It is through this body we get the occasional glimpse of the spiritual realms vouchsafed to the great souls of humanity ; through which we contact " the music of the spheres " ; and through which all that is finest and deepest in life is experienced. It is the body that brings us all really *authentic* religious moods and ecstasies, too (as opposed to the mere emotionalism which passes for such in the everyday world), as will be now readily understood by the reader ; and is indeed the gateway to that higher life and reality we all have vague intuitions of deep within ourselves.

In contradistinction to the intuitional body, the mental body is the seat of mundane thought ; the home of reason and logic, unlit by the fires of the intuition. It is in the mental body that the vast majority of scientists and thinkers reside, although the greatest of them have occasional flashes of inspiration from the intuitional body which marks them off from the rest of their kind as the real pioneers in their special fields of study. They are the real discoverers, and the great " pointers of the way " to their less intuitive confreres, whose work the latter tend to enclose in a sort of halo of sanctity, setting up the discoveries of the greater ones as dogmas to be worshipped by the lesser fry, exactly in the same way as the Churches have set up religious dogmas to be worshipped by erring man.

When the mental body is unlit by the fires from the intuitional, there is nothing but sterile thought as the result, the thought of our average scientist, philosopher, psychologist, and the like. These men do good work in their way, but it is uninspired and kills the spirit in whatever they are engaged on. It is very easy to see this in action in whatever special field of study one may be particularly interested in, once one's eyes are open to the fact, and it is precisely in being able to note this difference between inspired (or creative) and uncreative thought that the basic germ of true life-wisdom resides. When one can distinguish thought lit by inspiration and intuition from uninspired thought, in all its manifold variations and derivations, then one can claim to have truly taken a decisive step onwards along the path of true wisdom and life-knowledge.

The spiritual body is the home of the glorious spiritual power which is the very central core of our being. It is the origin of the inspiration and intuitional force which the intuitional body allows to filter down in flashes into the mental and lower bodies, to spur them to creative effort and achievement ; for we can have emotional inspiration (as in creative music and art, generally), and physical inspiration (as in dancing, and work with the hands and body, generally) as well as mental. Thus, all the various bodies (or principles) play their part in the life of the slowly evolving entity, man, and by knowing what is involved in it all, and consciously striving to co-operate with the forces at work within us *intelligently*, we can forward our evolution at a rate far surpassing that of those who stumble along blindly, unaware of what is going on, and becoming the sport and play of factors which control them instead of being controlled by them. The seventh body (the highest) we cannot hope to contact in our present stage of evolution, but it is the mainspring of everything within us, as already indicated. The more we evolve up the ladder of life, through successive incarnations, the more we make it possible for its force to come down to us and ennoble and inspirit us in everything we do.

Thus the sevenfold constitution of man can be likened to a miniature cosmos, each world working in its own way but united to all the rest in one common purpose and destiny. Man, the centre of this miniature cosmos, can achieve his crowning apotheosis and glory, as man, by understanding what is precisely the involved being he comprises, and ever striving to make himself into a fitter channel for the reception and dissemination of those forces from his Higher Self which radiate through him on all planes of his being. *Know thyself* is the old Delphic saying, and by knowing oneself through the knowledge of the seven principles, man can achieve his true liberation and destiny.

CHAPTER V

LIFE AFTER DEATH

THE spread of Scientific Materialism during the nineteenth century undermined Western man's faith in a life beyond the grave, as postulated by orthodox religion. Although no doubt there are many people who still cling to the belief in a life after death as understood in Church Christianity, modern man in the Western World finds the future chill and numb when he contemplates the declining years of his life. With hope of a life in the hereafter denied him by the " scientific " rulers of his mental outlook, and with no real inner faith to set up against the nihilism which encompasses him on all sides, he feels indeed lost and forlorn, an outcast in a Universe which has neither meaning nor purpose for him. No wonder he is beset by inner conflict and is the prey to nervous disorders of all kinds!

Yet, despite this depressing mental attitude regarding *post mortem* existence common nowadays to Western mankind as a whole, there is an undercurrent at work bringing hope to many millions in all parts of the world, who have found in Spiritualism an avenue through which to gain a glimpse of a world beyond the grave, which gives them encouragement to face the perils and pitfalls of existence with hope and fortitude.

But, from the Theosophical point of view, Spiritualism is far from being a true answer to man's quest for enlightenment as to the problems contained in the seeming eternal enigma of birth and death. The hidden world which is opened up to the enquirer into Spiritualism through a study of Spiritualist literature, or attendance at séances, is far too shallow and restricted, because Spiritualism deals only with that phase of the after-death state when the physical vehicle has been discarded, and the entity finds itself in the astral world, preparatory to passing on into the higher realms of discarnate existence after the " second death " (as it is occultly called) has taken place, and the last remaining vestiges of astral functioning have been brought to a close. The reader may remember that we said in the previous chapter that, when the physical body dies, the etheric body disintegrates concurrently with it, leaving the emotional and mental bodies to carry on for a time, quite intact, in the after-death state.

It is the breaking down of the particles of the emotional and mental bodies that takes place in that astral world referred to above, which is the second death in question, after which the finer essences of the emotional and mental life of the deceased are taken up by the Ego into its own realm in the intuitional world, to be worked into the Ego's *own nature*, thereafter to become permanent features of the being in question. In other words, all that is best in the emotional and mental life of the dead man are taken into permanent keeping by the Ego at the " second death " (to be dealt with more fully later), because they are the distilled essence, as it were, of the previous earth existence.

The remaining vestiges of the emotional and mental bodies are allowed to decay into their component units of emotional and mental matter in the astral world. So that when Spiritualism displays to us its version of life after death, or life beyond the grave, it is only giving us a view of that life which takes place *between the death of the physical body and the death of the emotional and mental bodies*. It shows us nothing of the higher life of the Ego in its own realms, because it knows nothing of such existence. Hence its denial of reincarnation. (There is no more stubborn opponent of the doctrine of *Reincarnation* than the average Spiritualist.)*

We do not wish to denigrate Spiritualism ; there are many earnest and sincere folk within the Spiritualist fold, and it has done good in many instances by making it possible for people to become *really convinced* that life continues unbroken, after the demise of the physical body.

In the modern world, with its disbelief in anything spiritual, it is indeed most encouraging to have this faith in a life beyond the grave established firmly in many minds and hearts. Spiritualism has done this work for a century, now, in the Western World, and we would be the last to try to minimize the value of such an

---

* The Spiritualism of Lord Dowding is of a much higher quality and *does* embrace reincarnation. It is Spiritualism of an entirely different order and type.

achievement. But in spiritualist literature the life painted as taking place after physical death is inexpressibly crude and meaningless, when compared with the light thrown on the subject through a study of Theosophy. We therefore feel it our bounden duty not to allow the present reader to fall into the trap so many have fallen into as a result of coming into touch with Spiritualism.

To the Spiritualist, one goes on living after physical death in a world which is practically identical with the one just departed from, with the same kind of thoughts and feelings, and the same kind of hopes and desires, but without having to fend for the physical organism as in earth life, and in surroundings usually pleasant and harmonious. It is what is known as the " Summerland " and there is no doubt a period of *post mortem* existence which can correspond to it, very largely, in the after-death experiences of many passing over that threshold which divides life from death, as we mortals see it.

But, as already stressed, the life in the astral realm portrayed to us by Spiritualism is only just *a phase* in the experiences passed through by the Ego and its bodies once the physical body has been discarded. To make it the final and complete consummation of earth-life that the spiritualist does, is therefore to proclaim once and for all his total lack of understanding of the whole problem. It cuts him off from any full realization of what life after death *really means* to man, and leaves him satisfied with a picture of events only a travesty of the true situation.

The " messages " and " voices " that come to him through the mediumistic séance, and which bring such comfort to him (because showing him that loved ones—although departed from earth-life—are still happy and contented in a world beyond the grave), are but the mere shadow-shows of astral happenings, did he but know it, and as far removed from actual communication with the dead as listening to the gramophone is like listening to the voice of the person making the record. In view of the extreme happiness such so-called communing with the dead gives to many bereaved ones, it is doubtless somewhat heartless to destroy their fond illusions ; but it would be doing the reader a disservice if **we** did not put before him the matter in its true perspective. Which is what we shall now try to do.

When an individual dies, it means merely, as already emphasized, that his physical body has been cast off, taking with it the etheric body and the vital essence which kept these two bodies functioning in the physical realm. But the emotional and mental bodies still carry on their functioning exactly as in earth-life, because the impulses created in those bodies during physical existence have to run their course and be expended, before the matter composing these bodies will be in a condition to allow of its disintegration into its component particles (as the physical and etheric bodies have already disintegrated into their component particles).

The final breaking up of the emotional and mental bodies in that after-death state we have called the astral world, does not take place until all the varied and jumbled thoughts and emotions which held the dead man in their thrall have been allowed to work out their momentum, as it were; for it is impossible for the matter composing the emotional and mental bodies to begin to disintegrate while under the tension imposed upon it by the thoughts and feelings in question.

That is to say, the dominant motives in the mind and heart of the individual who has passed through the gates of physical death will still dominate his life in the after-death state, so that all thoughts and feelings of a destructive—i.e. unethical, immoral, anti-social, etc.—nature, such as hatred, lust, feelings of revenge, greed, selfishness and the like, will still harass and prey on him for scores of years, perhaps, until their force has finally expended itself, when the unfortunate victim will at last be free of this incubus. The torment and suffering passed through by such an individual in the astral world is strictly *karmic* in character, being in direct ratio to the force and intensity of the retrograde and harmful thoughts and emotions experienced by him prior to death.

When this karmic retribution has been finally worked out on the deceased, in the after-death state, the bodies in which those thoughts and emotions had had lodgment, i.e. the emotional and mental bodies, will at last be ready for *their* death, as the physical and etheric bodies long since had passed through their demise and decay. It is this phase of the *post mortem* existence which we have already referred to as the " second death," for here the

Ego finally throws off the now outused emotional and mental garments previously worn through the whole period of incarnation.

As just made clear, all retrograde and harmful thoughts and emotions will have had their essence purged out of them during the sojourn in the astral world, the deceased man having to live over and over again, ceaselessly, until this expiation has been finally achieved, all the—among other things—selfish desires and longings held by him in earth-life, without having the physical body wherewith to grant them satisfaction, and accompanied by much remorse and bitter self-accusation in those capable of such feelings, especially in relation to previous evil deeds now gone over again and again in retrospect until they, too, have finally had their essence purged from consciousness. This is, indeed, the purgatory spoken of in the Christian Bible, and is in fact the only kind of " Hell " that man can really experience, being a hell purely of his own devising, because it is made up of the pangs and sufferings brought upon himself during this running down of the force and tension contained in the discreditable and evil thoughts and feelings possessed by him prior to physical death. Man suffers in this way, if he has had strong enough thoughts and feelings to warrant such a destiny. But, if he has lived a reasonably good life he is spared most of such torment in the astral realm, for there will be very little need of this "atonement of suffering" before the selfish wishes and coarse desires associated with his mental and emotional life have been worked off.

Thus, *Karma* sees that justice is fulfilled even beyond the grave, as countless numbers of evildoers have found to their cost. They may have escaped human justice through cunning and trickery, but Divine Justice can never be baulked, both as regards penalties in future earth-lives, and, as just seen, in *post mortem* existence, too.

We have so far dealt with the negative side of the after-death state: with the detrimental thoughts and feelings and the evil deeds which may have kept a man in their thrall and poisoned his life during earthly existence, to be expiated in the manner above referred to in the astral world. But what about man's *positive* thoughts and emotions and achievements? His constructive, creative, and humanly beneficial aspirations, actions, and the like? These factors in the mental and emotional life of the deceased constitute that essence of the mental and emotional make-up of the one who has passed over which we said previously were taken up by the Ego into its own realm, to be worked into the very fabric of being of the one concerned.

It is these thoughts, feelings, aspirations, and actions which constitute the very core and significance of his physical life on earth, and are what he has gleaned of worth from earthly existence in the incarnation just brought to a close. They will be worked into future character and innate quality, to be expressed afresh, under new conditions, during the next earthly incarnation.

Therefore, on the one hand we have the working out in the astral spheres of the dominant destructive thoughts, feelings, and actions of the previous earth-life, under strict Karmic control, bringing much pain and suffering (of a mental and emotional nature only, of course, but all the more intense for that) to the one going through that unhappy experience, until all inner tension and destructive vibratory effect has been worked out of the mental and emotional bodies.

On the other hand we have the distilled essence of all good and aspiring thoughts and feelings and actions taken up by the Ego into its own realm, i.e. the intuitional plane, leaving just the dregs of the emotional and mental bodies to rot and disintegrate into their component particles in the astral world. It is this condition, when reached, we have referred to as the " second death," after which what was left of *value* of the deceased is in the sole charge and keeping of the Ego in its own sphere. The dregs of emotional and mental matter on their way to final decay continue their existence in the astral world for some time still, the period depending essentially upon the strength of cohesion and toughness of the matter concerned.

It is *this decaying remnant of the outworn emotional and mental garment of the dead man which is what is usually contacted in the séance room.* The mediumistic séance has the power to attract such decaying and disintegrating entities (" shells " as they are called in occult literature), if the bond be strong enough ;

and it is from such astral corpses (as they really are) that we obtain the comforting messages and astral voices dear to the heart of spiritualists. There is a dying dynamic relationship still existing between the astral cadavers and the real entity (now passed on into the intuitional world), and it is quite possible for past experiences and thoughts to be brought to light and made to form those communications from the departed (usually trite and uninspiring, indeed, banal) we frequently hear in the séance room.

Often, of course, the messages are only the unconscious thoughts, feelings, and wishes of those desiring to contact the departed, brought to the surface through the medium's own nature, which is extremely susceptible and receptive to such thoughts and feelings and wishes ; but in many instances there is real contact with the one who has passed over, *but only with his dying astral shadow*, as just made clear. There is a great deal more that could be said on this subject, of interest to many nowadays, but the reader must be referred to the more advanced Theosophical literature for further investigation and enlightenment. We feel the purpose of the present book has been served by going into the matter to the extent we have.

There *is* a possibility (rather rare, however), that the real entity who has passed over can be contacted in the after-death state, and we do not rule it out of some spiritualist experiences of a very advanced type. This also is something which must be left to the student, however, to learn about in the more recondite Theosophical works. Speaking generally, it is the worst thing possible to *try* to get into communication with the dead, even from the best of motives. It only delays their passage through the astral world, and hinders them in their working out of those aspects of *post mortem* existence which have to be passed through before being ready to negotiate the " second death " and enter the world of the Ego.

The world of the Ego is the " Heaven World " (*Devachan*, in Sanskrit), and in its stay there the entity passes through a phase of exquisite enjoyment and bliss, working out the full implications of all that was best and most beautiful in earth existence, in the way of thought, feeling, aspiration, and action.

That is to say, whatever experiences of a constructive, altruistic, and creative nature the dead man had during earth-life, are worked out to the full in the " Heaven World " as Karmic repayment for being the possessor (or creator) of such thoughts, feelings, aspirations and actions.

We can see therefore that the ancient idea of " Heaven and Hell " has a great deal of truth in it, however distorted it has become during the ages. We *do* literally experience heaven and hell in the *post mortem* world, because all that is bad in our nature has to be worked off (expiated) in the astral realm ; while all that is good in our nature has its full realization and apotheosis in the Heaven World or *Devachan.*

Thus heaven and hell are realities in the cosmic life of man, but not as eternities, where one stays as a result of one life wisely or unwisely spent, as crudely represented in the Christian and other religions. They are phases in the life beyond the grave which the dying man passes through in strict accordance with the dominant tendencies displayed in the previous earth existence, prior to incarnating again in a new physical body.

At the expiry of the stay in the *Devachan* (a period which will naturally vary with the fullness and intensity of the type of life of thought and feeling of the deceased), the Ego will feel the urge for a new pilgrimage into earth existence (under Karmic pressure). It will descend again through the mental and emotional planes into the physical, taking with it fresh bodies of mental, emotional, etheric and physical matter, each such body being composed of the previously cast-off particles of such matter, which have been re-attracted to the reincarnating entity again through dynamic vibratory magnetic action. But the new bodies, although composed of the same material as the old, will not necessarily be like them. Everything will depend upon the life previously led in the various realms of matter, i.e., upon the way the physical body had been treated ; upon the way the emotional and mental life had been led. Thus we pass on from incarnation to incarnation with the threads of the past always woven into the present, under the stress of Karmic destiny, and thus a new being takes shape in the physical world to begin earth-life all over again.

It should be noted that although the beginning of physical life is at conception, the Ego has already gathered around it its mental, emotional and etheric bodies before the physical body has begun to develop (in its mother's womb). Conception is *not*, therefore, the start of the new life, as would be logical to assume from purely materialistic reasoning. It is the end-process in a chain of causation which reaches far back into the hidden and unseen, i.e., right back into the life of the Ego on its own plane. The Ego decides when it is time for reincarnation to be established, and it is *after this* that the physical foundation is laid for its new physical-plane habitat. All of which needs fuller elucidation for the reader in the more comprehensive Theosophical literature.

Of course, all that we have been trying to depict here for the newcomer to Theosophy in regard to life in the after-death world is extremely difficult to put into simple language. We must be forgiven, therefore, if some things have been made to appear more simple than is really the case. Otherwise it would not have been possible to bring home to the reader quite so clearly those basic elements of *post mortem* existence the present chapter was intended to portray. We feel that, on the whole, we have given a perfectly reliable and authentic account of the after-death state, whatever its limitations and omissions may be in certain directions. If the new student is overwhelmed by the wonder and mystery of it all, *well so are we, too*! It seems quite sacrilegious to try to deal with such subjects in a seemingly trite manner, but the attempt must be made, nevertheless, if any new light is to be vouchsafed to a world sunk in the gloom of Scientific Materialism and its denial of the spiritual side of human existence.

It will be noted that, in our references to Spiritualism, we showed that the spiritualist confuses the shadow with the substance in the after-death world ; and this is a point of major importance. The frequenter of séances contacts only the departing Mr. Jones or Mrs. Smith in so far as these entities are still clothed in the garments of the emotional and mental bodies, and then only when in the last stages of disintegration. He—the spiritualist —knows nothing of the existence of the Ego, which in itself has nothing to do with mere personalities of the Jones or Smith type, although using such personalities as factors in its pilgrimage through eternity. The spiritualist confuses the personality with the *real being*, and, having lost sight of this real being, denies it has any validity! Hence the stubborn opposition to the possibility of reincarnation in spiritualist literature already referred to.

The astral world, with its decaying astral corpses, is the be-all and end-all of existence so far as the spiritualist can see, and it is indeed a pity that such blindness is evinced by many in the spiritualist fold. H. P. Blavatsky came to the Western World not only to liberate mankind from Western Materialism and Scientific and Religious dogmatism; she also came to liberate Western man from the snares and pitfalls of Spiritualism. Many have called her a charlatan and fraud, not only because of her belief in the hidden side of things, but also because of her denouncement of the half-truths of spiritualist phenomena and manifestations. She has thus been vilified and defamed both by the scientific and orthodox religious, and by those who have had their spiritualist dreams rudely shattered by her dynamic personality and forceful tongue and pen. But it is essential to go on shattering the illusions of Spiritualism, for until this is accomplished there will be millions of people who will be unable to take the essential step for them to be able to embrace the Theosophical philosophy, which can really help them to an understanding of the enigma of life beyond the grave.

Special Note. In this chapter on life after death we have made no reference to suicide, murder and sudden death, generally. This aspect of the matter is, of course, dealt with fully in the more advanced Theosophical literature, and has many special problems. Here we can say only that if someone commits suicide, he does not thereby escape the results of his action by shuffling off the physical body; far from it. In the astral world he relives over and over again the suicidal act, together with the factors which led to this dread step; so that the suicide learns all to his cost, when it is too late, that it does not pay in the least to try to shirk life's responsibilities. Of course, in every case of suicide it will naturally depend (as to the effects of the act on the individual in the after-death state), upon the chief motive operating in the taking of the life. Motive is everything, here, in assess-

LIFE AFTER DEATH

ing the results of such action. The murderer who is hanged as punishment for his crime also lives on in the astral world to poison the atmosphere with his thoughts and feelings. The cessation of physical life is far from being the end for him, too, as well as for the society which sent him to his fate. There is a great deal that the new student will have to learn, on these subjects, in more advanced studies.

CHAPTER VI

THE HIERARCHICAL STRUCTURE OF THE UNIVERSE

IN this chapter we come to a subject that is very difficult for the Western mind to grasp, because it is so foreign to Western modes of thought. In the West (at least as far as democratic countries are concerned), we regard man as being a free agent, able to live his life exactly as he chooses, as far as his circumstances—physical, mental, social, environmental, and financial—will allow. Man can do what he wishes with his life, except that he has to live that life within the framework of the laws of the country of which he is a citizen. If he chooses to live that life for pleasure, or for the amassing of wealth, or for the good of his fellows, it is left entirely to his own initiative, and is regarded as nobody's concern but his own.

In recent years, this democratic view of man's life has been rather rudely shattered by the spread of the doctrines of Communism and Fascism. Although the latter gospel has been badly battered in the late war, and its main tenets scattered in the dust, as it were, the former lives on more stoutly than ever as a result of the same world-wide cataclysm of man-made death and destruction, and is steadily becoming a greater menace to all lovers of the democratic way of living. Personally, we can see very little essential difference between Communism and Fascism, although they are superficially so much unlike each other. In both systems there is dictatorship from above, the individual becoming the tool and servant of the State, and having no free life of his own, being regarded as so much human material for use in furthering the ends of the country of which he happens to be a national. The citizen living under a dictatorship of the Right or Left has no real say in the ordering of his life (as regards its larger aspects) and owes implicit and complete allegiance to the ruler of the State Machine.

Naturally, under both Communism and Fascism, there were

THE HIERARCHICAL STRUCTURE 75

and are certain definite advantages accruing to such subjects of totalitarian rule, as compared with the members of a democratic state. But man's most prized possession—his individual freedom—has been filched from him, and, in the eyes of the Western World, generally, there could be no greater crime. Indeed, we may say that, as a general axiom, *Western man values his freedom more than his life,* however greater social and economic factors may conspire to prevent the attainment of his dreams and aspirations.

In turning now to the subject of the present chapter, i.e., the hierarchical structure of the Universe, we come face to face with a situation which, although seeming to parallel, in many aspects, the Communist and Fascist view of the place and status of the individual in society, is, nevertheless, in full harmony and accord with the truly democratic ideals and principles which regard as transcendental realities the freedom of the subject and his basic right to make what he likes of his life within the framework of the community of which he is a component member.

The essential factor in the rulership principle which governs the Universe, and now about to be discussed, is *leadership from above combined with the fullest possible degree of individual freedom and initiative below,* achieved by the graded devolution of duties and services from those higher in the hierarchical structure to those lower, stretching in an unending and unbroken line from the highest unit to the lowest in the Universal Whole. This is certainly a rather breath-taking spectacle of graded universal planning and co-ordination to set before the reader, but without such planning and co-ordination the world as we know it would not continue for one day or even one minute.

It is only by such inter-relationship and integration of duties covering the whole Cosmical Scheme, in graded series of importance of function, under the charge, at every focal point, of a being (or entity) who, in turn, forms one of a higher grade of entities under the charge of a being yet more fully advanced up the hierarchical scale, that universal life is able to go on with such seeming effortlessness and ease. It is a vast Cosmical Machine of wheels within wheels, stretching to the farthest horizon.

Let us try to make the position somewhat clearer in the reader's mind by taking the human body as an illustration. Here we have an entity composed of countless millions of cells, made up (through graded series of cell activity) into various organs and structures, all of which organs and structures have their own special individual purpose and function to perform in the economy of the whole, yet which together make up that whole, by their united effort. The various organs and structures live their own personal lives, so to speak, but only within the framework of the larger life of the human entity of which they form part.

Thus we see at a glance what hierarchical structure really is, and how, under it, each component has its own freedom of action, but within the larger pattern of the total organism, which encompasses each individual unit, *and gives its work meaning and significance*. (Note this latter phrase carefully. It supplies the clue to the answer to that most vexed question of the meaning and purpose of created life, generally.)

As is now clear (we hope), each individual unit and component in the human organism *has its own life to live, in its own special way*, within the framework of larger and larger groups of units, which larger groups, in turn, form part of yet larger units, and so on up and up to the complete body itself, functioning as a united whole. But, unless each individual unit or component lives its life in full conformity with its *own innate characteristics*, and does not try to live otherwise (the brain not trying to usurp the functions of the heart or liver, for instance ; or the kidneys those of the lungs) then the total aggregate of units—the human organism—is unable to carry out its necessary tasks as perfectly as it should do, and so each individual unit or component suffers accordingly. In other words, unless each unit of the human machine functions to the very best of its ability in the special task it has been accorded in the human economy, each and every unit will suffer through the inharmony and inadequacy of the whole.

That, in a nutshell, expresses the tremendous significance to man of the Theosophical doctrine we are attempting to make clear to the reader in the present chapter. Its importance cannot be over-estimated in relation to the problems of human welfare and happiness.

For, just as each unit of the human organism can only fulfil

THE HIERARCHICAL STRUCTURE

its function—and so derive its greatest satisfaction from living —by being *itself* and not trying to be something else, thereby assuring the full and harmonious functioning of the entire human entity, so man is a unit of a being greater than himself, and can only achieve his fullest happiness and destiny by attempting to become that being he is intended to be within the framework of that larger whole (Mankind). Whereas, however, the units of the human body have no wish (or opportunity, we may say) to be anything different from what they were originally intended to be, man, through his mental apparatus, can desire and long for things which may not be—and mostly are not—what he should desire and long for. Hence the whole (of which man forms part) fails to function as it should do, with the resultant chaos of our times.

Naturally, within the larger unit of mankind there are smaller units of nation, race, community, tribe, township, village, and so forth. It is because man has lost the secret of functioning consciously as a fully co-operative unit within each of such smaller frameworks, that he finds himself unable to live as completely and satisfactorily as he would like to in the world of to-day. His conscious mind pushes him in certain directions, governed by selfishness, lust, greed, etc., and perverts the functioning of his basic instincts and intuitions, upon which the animal and lower kingdoms rely implicitly for guidance, thereby ensuring that they, when not interfered with by man and his civilizing processes, still live harmoniously within the framework of the larger life of which they form a part, while *homo sapiens* (the reputed master of all!) does not. Of course, if we trace back the causes far enough, we shall find the civilizing process *itself* at the root of man's troubles in living, which does not necessarily mean that civilization as such is wrong, but only man's development of it.

Error has been piled upon error, as the centuries of civilized living have passed, until to-day modern Western man is quite unable to find any meaning or purpose in existence and so seeks vainly for guidance and leadership. It will be only when he turns for such guidance and leadership *within himself* (to the Ego, which knows full well its destiny and purpose, and has never lost touch with its divine source as has the purely personal self), that he will find the way out of his difficulties, and so solve his present seemingly insurmountable problems in living. Man, by discovering his *real self*, will thereby also discover the meaning and purpose of his existence, and thus automatically find his place and fulfil his function within the Universal Hierarchical Whole.

The Hierarchical Structure of the Universe naturally embraces within itself the Earth, too, upon which mankind lives. It also is part of something greater than itself, i.e., the Solar System, within which it has its allotted function and purpose to perform. The Solar System, in turn, has its own allotted function and purpose to perform within the greater entity—the Galactic System—of which it forms a unit, and so on right through the whole vast cosmical structure, the complete Universal Aggregate.

Each component particle of that vast congeries of beings, forces and constellations—stretching in unbroken series from the atom at the one end to the Creators of Cosmoi at the other—has its rightful task and function to fulfil within the framework of the Total Universal Entity (as well as within the pattern of varying lesser frameworks and entities, according to its position within the Hierarchical Scale), the whole being vivified by the force and energy of the CENTRAL SOURCE OF ALL LIFE at the centre of this colossal network of pulsating activity of spirit and matter.

From the CENTRAL SOURCE OF ALL radiates the inspiration which keeps everything in being and motion, and, as each step downwards into lower spheres of activity and manifestation is taken, beings of requisite magnitude and power control each phase of the stepping-down process, each looking to the one above for inspiration and guidance, but being entirely responsible for the effective working of the universal unit of which it is in command.

Thus we find the machinery of the Universe controlled at every stage of its functioning by beings and agencies which, looking above for guidance, oversee lesser beings or agencies or forces below themselves, at the same time being in sole command of *their own special task or sphere of activity*, thus forming a vast network (a gargantuan cobweb of universal magnitude) which embraces every single animate and inanimate object in the Universe within its orbit.

The one below looks to the one above for inspiration and

guidance in the hierarchical scheme, we have said, but that does not mean that all independent thought and initiative is relinquished thereby. On the contrary. Here we come to that fundamental difference between the governing principle of the hierarchical system and the totalitarian systems referred to in the opening paragraphs of this chapter.

In such totalitarian systems man has his individual freedom and initiative filched from him within the framework of the State Machine of which he forms one cog, whether small or large, according to his special circumstances. He looks to those in authority for his orders and works within the rigid circle of his set task or function. Any attempt to develop his own innate personal qualities at the expense of the State Octopus that holds him within its grasp is not only frowned upon: it may be dangerous to his life. One " toes the party line "—or else . . . !

Under the hierarchical system, however, every single unit in the vast scheme is not only allowed *but expected* to develop his innate qualities and capacities to the full. It is precisely through such development of qualities and capacities that each component in the universal whole attains its fullest functional perfection and allows for the progressively better functioning of the total organism.

Thus, although it may seem superficially that authoritarianism has much in common with hierarchical devolution of duties, because those below certainly do look to those above for guidance under both systems, one allows for the fullest personal freedom of development (within the framework of the total organization), whereas the other stultifies personal initiative and character, sacrificing everything not of value to its ordained mode of conduct and behaviour *to its own ends*.

Man, therefore, as a unit in the Hierarchical Scheme, does not lose any of his innate personal freedom by being an integral part of the total Universal Mechanism, although superficially seeming to do so. On the contrary, he gains immeasurably thereby, because within it and through it ONLY can he find his complete fulfilment AS MAN. (A point that will be brought out more fully in the next chapter.)

The 100 per cent democratic ideal of complete freedom of the individual without restraints of any kind fails to be entirely satisfactory, because under it some people rise to the top through the expression of their innate powers and capacities, while others of their fellows sink to the bottom, their boasted freedom set at nought by enslaving economic factors, to be made tools of by those with greater ability than themselves. The totalitarian systems rectify this situation in certain aspects, *at the expense of the freedom of all.* The hierarchical system, on the other hand, incorporates what is best in *both* types of development, it will now be seen, and is indeed the model upon which all government, whether of states or of the world as a whole, should be planned. Until we achieve this condition of freedom for all, within a framework of planned and integrated development embracing the entire globe, and aiming at the release *of the true spirit of man,* no type of government, no matter of what kind, will succeed in making humanity really contended and happy in the world it inhabits.

This is a lesson all statesmen *must* learn in order to establish real world harmony and concord, and such tentative beginnings as the " League of Nations " or the " United Nations " are but the veriest child's steps along the path that must be trodden by modern man. This shows that the hierarchical pattern is intended to be followed by all categories of beings or entities because it is the only pattern which has the stamp of universal approval.

In the Bible we read of Dominions, Powers, and Principalities ; the Arch-Angels, Angels, Seraphim and Cherubim, etc. These are all titles of Great Beings in charge of certain stages or spheres of Universal Hierarchical Structure ; (of Globes, Planets, Solar Systems, various types of evolutionary development, and the like). The " Masters of Wisdom " referred to in an earlier chapter (two of whom were the founders of the Theosophical Society through their agent, Madame Blavatsky), are also essential links in the hierarchical chain, being one stage more progressed than ordinary mortals such as ourselves, and connecting us—through them—with the Great Beings who have charge of the destiny of the human race and of this globe. These Great Beings, in turn, are part of a greater order of beings or powers which connect our globe and humanity with greater patterns of cosmical evolutionary activity and development, and so on. The picture thus opened up to the discerning eye is full of the utmost grandeur and significance, showing us that we are linked through and through with the Universe in its inherent development and destiny, and taking an essential part in that development and destiny ; an unconscious part for most of us, at present, but an increasingly conscious and purposeful part the more we come to know of the Theosophical teachings.

We have said that the Masters of Wisdom link man with higher stages of evolutionary development, and, of course, man is a step above the animal world which is the link between us and the plant and mineral kingdoms below (this will be gone into more fully in the next chapter). But there are also hosts of *invisible* kingdoms of entities carrying on their essential parts in the hierarchical functioning of the Universe, which the more recondite Theosophical literature will make clear to the reader. It would be too much to attempt to go into that aspect of the subject here.

If we have revealed in the present chapter something of the nature of the vast Hierarchical Structure which underlies all cosmical existence, and which encompasses man within its orbit, too, we feel that our task has been accomplished. The key to it all is: *infinite diversity within unity,* each unit linked inseparably to every other, and each achieving its fullest development and realizing its essential purpose and significance by the carrying out of its own allotted part of the universal plan in the manner laid down by the Great Architects ruling the spheres, acting as the lieutenants of the *Ineffable Source of All.* A truly noble idea and ideal, of which mankind must learn the nature and essential meaning in order to achieve real fulfilment for man in the world we inhabit.

F

CHAPTER VII

CREATIVE EVOLUTION AND THE DOCTRINE OF SWABHÂVA

WHEN Charles Darwin published his epoch-making book *The Origin of Species*, just about a century ago, and the idea of Evolution was first brought to the notice of Western thinkers, its impact upon the thought of his day was profound, to say the least. *Instead of man being a special creation of God, as heretofore assumed, henceforth he was nothing but a glorified animal, descended from the animal kingdom through the agency of the ape, who was thus reputed to be man's direct ancestor!* The controversy that then raged throughout Western Civilization, between Church and Science, was bitter in the extreme.

It was from that period onward that the hitherto unchallenged authority of Orthodox Religion began to wane. Many and protracted were the conflicts between leading divines and outstanding men of science over the vexed question of the origin of man. The Darwinians won, however, all along the line, and the Church had to retire from the fray, very much battered in open warfare, with Western man proudly announcing to all and sundry that he was "descended from the monkey." (Although where pride is concerned we fail to see!) But such was the jubilation of Science in having worsted Authoritarian Religion, that it was ready to accept the monkey as lineal ancestor with resigned satisfaction, so long as it had scored momentously over the religious pundits of the day.

Darwinian Evolution still dominates the thought of Western man, as it began to do a century ago, although many of Darwin's leading assumptions have never been verified, and indeed have been disproved by certain anthropologists and others. The results of this dominance are gradually but surely making themselves felt.

In his glee at having scored heavily over the supporters of orthodox religion, the evolutionist did not quite realize that he

CREATIVE EVOLUTION

was thereby forfeiting all possibility of regarding himself as a being with a spiritual nature and heritage, one who was joined directly to his Maker through the unseen thread of the soul and spirit he was assumed to possess under orthodox religious teaching. Man threw away his spiritual birthright of divine union with God in the flush of his evolutionary enthusiasm, and was content to regard himself as a higher animal, the highest animal of them all, in fact!

The denial of biblical Christianity which generally followed in the wake of the spread of the Darwinian Evolutionary Theory is well known, and much of the chaos and confusion of our times can be traced directly to that one source. Because, denying any connection with anything spiritual inside and outside himself, Western man abandoned himself to the pursuit of material ends in an ever-increasing degree, the two devastating world wars of recent years being fitting outcomes of such a process.

But, although Darwin's Theory of the Evolution of Species has brought a lamentable result in its impact on the Western World, *Evolution* (as an integral feature of Cosmic existence) has been known in the East for untold ages past, as recorded in all ancient religions and philosophies (albeit often in a disguised form). The wonderful discovery that brought Western man to his knees, in admiration of the genius of Darwin, and which has revolutionized Western thought so momentously, was known for countless centuries in the esoteric schools and hidden religious teachings of the East, as stated above, *but with a difference of profound significance*!

According to the Darwinian view, evolution is a process which results from the impact of external events and conditions upon the myriad types of evolving species under the constant influence of such external stress and tension. And, according to the Darwinian Theory, it is the species that best withstand the constant onslaught of external conditions, favourable and unfavourable, which survive and pass on their characteristics—sharpened and enhanced through unceasing conflict with external Nature— to their offspring, thus bringing about the gradual transformation of one type or species into another, through the ages.

The fittest survive, and the weakest go to the wall, we are told, and thus has the mighty spectacle of evolution been carried on throughout countless epochs, bringing as its final consummation and apotheosis MAN, with his overlordship of all kingdoms lower than himself. The Darwinian Conceptions of "Nature Red in Tooth and Claw" and the "survival of the fittest" have naturally worked their way into the everyday thought of Western man. The introduction of such devilish atrocities into modern warfare as the atom bomb, germicidal warfare, poison gas, etc., can be traced directly to this source. Modern civilized man has been told that only the fittest survive, and he now takes that to mean: fittest in the art of developing methods of destroying his fellows! No longer is it a question of muscle and brawn, but of "back-room boys" working in secrecy to perfect evermore destructive methods of bringing death to their fellow human beings. To this pass has the Darwinian Theory of Evolution brought the world!

We have just said that evolution is an essential factor in the Cosmical Scheme, and its details were known in the religious and philosophical teachings of the ancients. But not as understood by modern Darwinians; *far otherwise*! Whereas to the Darwinian the emphasis in evolution lies essentially on the effect of external forces and conditions upon the evolving types, from the Eastern point of view the evolutionary emphasis is laid directly upon the inner spiritual life of the evolving entity.

The difference in outlook and thought is profound, and its effects are just as epoch-making. For in this divergence of views regarding the main causative factor in evolution lies the essential difference between Western and Eastern thought; the one denying the spirit and looking to material aims and ends; the other regarding the inner spiritual essence as all-important and looking upon material factors as of only minor significance.

When the Darwinian talks of the evolution of man from the amœba, through the plant and animal kingdoms, the picture he has before him is of *evolving forms,* of forms or bodies gradually showing more and more signs of conscious characteristics, and with greater and greater powers of fending for themselves in the world into which they are born. As evolution progresses, according to this conception, greater adaption to the external environment is the keynote of evolutionary development. The way upwards from amœba to man is strewn with the corpses of countless species of extinct and living forms, through which a pattern of gradually increasing conscious striving and adaptability can be discerned.

That is the view of evolution put before us by the Darwinian, and it is characterized by a complete absence of any indication of spiritual factors being concerned in the evolutionary process. According to this standpoint evolution is essentially *materialistic,* being the outcome of the interaction of external forces and factors with the *evolving form*. Why such a process should result in the production of higher and higher types of entities, culminating in Man, the Darwinist is quite unable to say.

The whole thing is purely the outcome of luck or chance, he will tell you, and that is all there is to it, as far as he is concerned. To such a degree has Western thought degraded itself. To such views, bankrupt of all spiritual content, is it firmly wedded. It never seems to occur to scientific thinkers to wonder how a form can react to external stimuli if there is nothing *vital and self-adaptative inside it* capable of making such a reaction. If there is nothing within to react to the external pressure or stimulus through the medium of the form it inhabits, surely there can never be the slightest possibility of change of any kind? There would be just a static world of unchanging forms, fossilized units of living matter, little different from the mineral kingdom, except able to eat and propagate their kind. Incidentally, how could such entities even be able to eat and propagate their kind if there was not some guide or mentor inside them capable of directing such profoundly decisive processes? Surely instincts of such immense biological significance do not arise by mere accident or chance? Or do they?

To this sorry pass, then, is the Darwinist reduced, when trying to look within the evolutionary edifice erected before an admiring audience during the past century. No wonder we live in an age racked by pessimism and doubt. All that is really vital in the evolutionary conception is carefully excluded from the Darwinian presentation of it. Western man goes on his way still thinking that luck and chance rule his life, and that it is a good thing that at least he has got rid of the tail of his tree-swinging simian ancestors!

If we now turn to the Eastern conception of evolution, with

its emphasis laid upon the inner evolving spirit and not upon the outward form, which is there regarded only as the physical instrument made use of by the entity within in its struggle with the external environment, in order to gain ever-fuller conscious self-expression for itself, *we see an entirely different picture.*

Instead of evolution being a meaningless and chance procedure, bereft of all significance, it now becomes something of vital importance because being the picture-story, as it were, of the gradual evolution of spirit through matter to ever-higher forms of conscious expression in the material world. We then see that each phase of the evolutionary process means the development of yet further degrees of innate spiritual and instinctive qualities, and that as each kingdom reaches its culmination, a yet higher kingdom of species begins to appear because activated by a more potent degree (or quantity) of inner spiritual energy.

Thus, evolution begins to take on meaning and purpose when viewed from the "inside" (as we are now looking at it) instead of from the "outside" (as the Darwinist views it). In short, evolution is seen for what it really is, i.e., the gradual development, through myriads of forms, species, and kingdoms of living entities, of ever-higher concentrations of spirit acting through matter (as its outward envelope), thus producing the force and sweep—ever onwards and upwards—of the evolutionary process, culminating, at our present stage of development on this globe, with man.

Man is the highest expression of inner spiritual forces and energies yet existent on the globe we inhabit, as discernible to mortal eye, and that is his true meaning and significance in the evolutionary plan. Just as there are kingdoms below man, so there are kingdoms above (as referred to in the previous chapter), but to the seeing mortal eye man is the highest pinnacle yet reached by the evolving spirit within.

Thus does the Eastern conception of Evolution dignify man, raising him spiritually and connecting him directly with the evolving spiritual forces working within and through him ; and thus is man given a position and status which can only ennoble him and raise him yet further spiritually, as he strives to make himself a conscious co-worker with the evolutionary process. What a difference from the Darwinian conception of evolution,

CREATIVE EVOLUTION

with its denial of anything spiritual in the nature of man, and its making of chance and luck the rulers of his destiny!

We are all acquainted with the various stages of evolutionary development from the lowest form of living matter, i.e., from the amœba (the single-celled organism) through the plants and fishes to the animal kingdom and man. From the Theosophical point of view these stages in evolutionary development are correct, except that instead of man being the decendant of the animal world through the agency of the monkey and ape, as Darwinism asserts, he is regarded as the *progenitor* of the animal evolution, and the ape and monkey as direct descendants of his (as a result of copulation between archaic man and certain primitive non-human types) aeons back in the far distant infancy of human development.

These views are no doubt rather startling to the mind of Western man, firmly versed, by this time, in the Darwinian view of things; but a study of the more advanced Theosophical literature will convince the reader of the soundness of these statements, although so strange and puzzling when first met. The point is that these matters relate to conditions when man was anything but what he is to-day, and the world he inhabited equally unlike the solid material-looking globe we now walk on. These events refer to epochs millions and millions of years back in the far distant history of evolving humanity.

Starting with the mineral kingdom (far from being purely material and inanimate, as orthodox science would have us believe, but pregnant with unexpressed life) we climb through the various stages of evolutionary development, each stage being a rung higher up the evolutionary ladder than the one below, through the plant and animal kingdoms, to man.

But, from the Theosophical point of view, evolution itself, through these various stages, could never have been possible unless the evolving life-spirit contained within the forms mentioned, which is seeking to achieve ever-fuller self-expression for itself through those forms, had not been first *involved into them*. In other words, before *evolution* can take place, i.e., the drawing out of inner potentiality and spiritual quality, there must be a prior process of *involution* of spirit into the forms capable of making evolutionary development.

That is another of the significant contributions of Theosophy (and Esoteric Philosophy, generally) to the subject under discussion. Darwinian Evolution disregards the inner evolving spirit and concentrates entirely upon the form. Eastern conceptions of Evolution, in general, stress the essential significance in the evolutionary process of the inner evolving spirit using the forms which evolve.

But the real esoteric teaching goes a step further and indicates that without a prior investing of the evolving entities themselves with the spiritual power capable of providing the urge for that evolutionary ascent through matter, which is what evolution essentially is, there could be no such thing as evolution. In other words, without an original *in-breathing* of spirit into matter, there could never be the possibility of any further *out-breathing* of such spirit through material forms, as takes place in the evolutionary scheme.

Thus does the Theosophical conception of evolution give the whole process an immeasurably wider scope and connotation, for we see in action in the evolutionary spectacle the very essence and impetus of UNIVERSAL CREATIVE LIFE ITSELF, coming from the Heart and Centre of all Existence.

The creative Life-Breath, as it may be termed, first involves itself in the most attenuated forms of matter, of which matter another aspect of the same Creative Life-Breath is also the progenitor, spirit-matter being one and indivisible throughout Creation, and being just different modes or aspects of the all-pervading activity of the self-same PRIMAL CREATIVE LIFE-ESSENCE. To realize the intensity and force of primal creative power required to formulate the material side of life, consider present-day research into atomic energy, bearing in mind that the atom is almost infinitesimal in size, yet has such an enormous energy-potential locked up in it. The first most tenuous kind of matter, invested with the elementary evolving life-breath, develops gradually into more complex matter under the impetus of the creative impulse working through it; and so on up through three grades (or kingdoms). These are known as the *first, second and third elemental kingdoms* in Theosophical literature. Passing through these, the mineral kingdom is reached, thence through the plant and animal creation to man. Thus we have *seven stages of evolving life* in the Theosophical portrayal of the evolutionary process, beginning with the first elemental kingdom and ending with man. (*Another septenary*.) This conception of the initial involution of spirit in matter and then of its gradual evolution through ever higher forms of material life as the spiritual impetus gains increasing momentum, is a most profound and thought-stimulating one indeed, as the reader can well see. What a contrast to the accepted Darwinian view! The two conceptions are poles apart, and aptly illustrate the immeasurable distance that divides Theosophy from modern Western thought, generally.

We have said that one aspect of the Creative Life-Breath is responsible for the formation of the matter providing the material vehicles which house the inner evolving spirit during the evolutionary process; the inner evolving spirit's involution in matter being itself the outcome of the activity of another aspect of the self-same all-pervading Creative Urge. But there is a third and vitally important phase in the evolutionary drama yet to be unfolded to the reader. That is something which takes place after the nascent human stage has been arrived at in evolutionary development.

What happens then is that man's Higher Self—his Egoic Consciousness—steps in to take possession of the primitive human form laboriously built up through the processes previously described. This is, indeed, a mystery of mysteries. It results from the activity of yet a third aspect of the same originating Creative Life-Essence working along another and higher line of development than the two to which we have previously referred. From the Darwinian point of view there is no essential difference between man and the animals except that he is a more cunning and intelligent type of animal. From the Theosophical standpoint, however, the essential distinguishing characteristic between man and the animals is that man has a definite *manifesting soul of his own, and the ability for conscious thought and constructive activity*, conferred by virtue of his possession of that Higher Self —or Egoic Consciousness—that came to him as a result of the action of the third and highest aspect of Primal Creative functioning just referred to, which has been taking place on a totally different plane from that of the lower evolutionary process.

In their state of evolution the animals have only a *latent* soul, no self-consciousness, and no power of constructive thinking; they have merely a rudimentary degree of intellectual development, and their spiritual consciousness is nil. The fundamental difference between man and the animal world is naturally of the profoundest significance, and explains why it is impossible for a man to be descended from the animal kingdom, even from the apes or monkeys as Darwinism postulates (although *on the form side* he is certainly a continuation of the lower evolutionary process). With regard to the simians, as already intimated they are hybrid descendants from the primitive human evolutionary stock, and can in no sense be regarded as anterior to man.

We thus find the evolutionary teachings of Theosophy completely revolutionary in outlook, as compared with current thought upon the subject. They confer upon man a significance which links him with the highest Creative Essence of the Universe, instead of relegating him to the position of a mere higher animal, with no spiritual nature whatsoever.

In view of all this the reader will perhaps wonder why the "World of Science" does not give its considered attention to the Theosophical viewpoint, being a body of people professedly always "seeking for the truth" in scientific matters. But it is surprising how loth scientists (or, rather, those with a supposedly scientific training and outlook) are to change pre-conceived theories and viewpoints which have moulded their thought for decades. The medical profession is an outstanding case in point in regard to not accepting unorthodox healing methods of proved value in the treatment of disease.

Thus, the profoundly important statements regarding the origin and development of man and the true nature and purpose of evolution are quietly ignored in scientific circles. They are considered as being incompatible with current evolutionary views, and any new discoveries deemed likely to enhance the unorthodox viewpoint are conveniently overlooked by having a "blind eye" turned upon them. (For further elaboration of this point, together with a very full analysis and discussion of the whole body of Theosophical teachings regarding evolution, the reader is referred to the book: *Man in Evolution,* by Gottfried de Purucker, a Theosophical classic.)

Again, from the orthodox evolutionary angle, man has been

in existence on this earth perhaps a few hundred thousand years. At first it was put at fifty thousand years or so, but the time has been expanded gradually, through anthropological discoveries, to a few hundred thousand of years. But from the Theosophical teachings we learn that mankind has been in existence on this planet for *many millions of years,* thereby enlarging enormously the canvas of the evolutionary picture, and incidentally solving many archaeological, ethnical, and anthropological problems in the process, problems unsolvable to the orthodox scientists who encompass the life of man within a span of a few hundreds of thousands of years.

Thus does Theosophy shed light and understanding all along the line, as it were, as we survey the evolutionary scene through its eyes. We are indeed fortunate, in the West, to have such knowledge given us for the asking, so to speak. But only those whose *Karma* makes them worthy are permitted to benefit therefrom, let it be fully understood! In other words, of the many who contact Theosophy in one way or another, relatively few are they whose destiny allows them to really absorb its teachings.

So much, then, for the general study of evolution, from the Theosophical angle. That is as far as we propose to take the matter in the present book. Now let us turn to the second part of this chapter, which has to deal with the esoteric doctrine of *Swabhâva.*

This is another profoundly illuminating Theosophical teaching, and its significance is of enormous personal value to all students, for reasons that will soon be made clear. We have said that the third (and highest) aspect of the Creative Life-Breath (working along an entirely different evolutionary line from its two lower aspects) has invested man with his unique soul or spirit, thereby marking him off from all other entities lower in the evolutionary scale, and also marking him off, incidentally, from all other human beings, too. Through this soul or spirit which links him with Divinity and which confers on him his essential SELFHOOD, every single human being is differentiated *for all Eternity* from all other human beings, living or dead.

It is this essential difference or uniqueness bestowed on every member of the human race by virtue of the soul or spirit which in his inner core, that links up with the doctrine of *Swabhâva* we now wish to talk about. For this doctrine—which is common to all esoteric teachings, generally—states that each evolving being has a special quality (or "flavour," we might say), which is especially and uniquely *his very own*, being his inmost essence, so to speak. It is his evolutionary destiny to bring out more and more fully this quality or flavour as he progresses onwards and upwards through the evolutionary cycle.

We all know that the distinguishing characteristic of an oak-tree (i.e., that which makes it an oak-tree and not anything else), is different entirely from that of a beech-tree, shall we say; and, likewise, the distinguishing characteristic of a cat (i.e., that which confers on it its "catness"), is essentially different from that which confers on a dog his "dogness." And it is this characteristic difference, resulting from the presence and action of the inner qualitative essence, which is what is being referred to when speaking about a thing's "*Swabhâva*" (its "Swabhâva" being the inner qualitative essence). We each have our own special *Swabhâva* which makes us *ourselves*; that distinguishes us from all other beings; that distinguishes brother from brother, and sister from sister within the same family group. During the evolutionary process it is our destiny (and indeed duty, once we are aware of the fact) to develop our *Swabhâva* so that we can become more and more fully *ourselves* as each incarnation passes.

The bird or animal is *itself* in so far as it obeys the instincts and impulses which make it what it is, within its own genus or species, and is thereby expressing its *Swabhâva*. But man— through the fact of having a soul or spirit of his own—is more than just a member of the human race, and cannot therefore rely solely on instinct and rudimentary impulse for the propulsive force necessary for the expression of his particular *Swabhâva*, as do the members of the lower kingdoms. That would merely keep him for ever at the savage level, i.e., a mere human animal. He must seek incessantly to develop his *Swabhâva* more and more, through incarnation after incarnation, by dint of ever-fuller conscious self-expression as man, as he progresses up the evolutionary ladder.

Although the process in question is largely instinctive and unconscious in the vast majority of people at present, it is nevertheless in operation in one form or another as they seek means of giving expression through work or creative activity to special aptitudes or proclivities they find themselves born with. It is indeed these special aptitudes and proclivities which give us the clue to our individual *swabhâvic* quality or flavour, as they are its outward expression in consciousness.

It is by seeking *consciously* to develop this *Swabhâva* of ours, once our eyes are open to its existence within us, that we can hasten on our own evolutionary development, and so at last play a really constructive part in the Cosmic Scheme of Things.

Until we are able to take this decisive step in co-operation, we are going merely with the tide, so to speak ; we are merely blind actors in the evolutionary drama, life after life. But once we *know* we have a certain *Swabhâva* of our very own, which it is incumbent upon us to bring forth and develop consciously, through our work, or general mode of living, then we become self-conscious co-workers with Nature, and at last make that step forward into the path of *self-directed evolution* which is the hall-mark of those human beings who, in the esoteric tradition, are spoken of as having *set their feet upon the path*.

We shall have more to say about this "Path" later in the present book, but at the moment we just wish to make it clear to the reader that it refers to a mode of living which brings the student more speedily up the evolutionary ladder than is possible to the average human being, who is content to be carried along in the main evolutionary current, as it were, without conscious co-operation of any kind on his part (through not knowing of the need for such co-operation or of the reason for its necessity).

Thus, by seeking to develop his *Swabhâva,* i.e., his inner qualities and aptitudes which mark him off from his fellows, man can hasten forward his evolutionary development very considerably, and at the same time he will be making himself a co-worker with Nature in the vast evolutionary scheme. He will cease to be a mere unconscious participant, but will henceforth become a being consciously directing his own evolutionary development with full understanding and determination.

He will know that by developing his *Swabhâva* he will be developing HIMSELF as fully as he possibly can, and thereby making himself that which he was originally intended to be by the Creative Life Essence, a particle of which are his soul and spirit. For, although it is true that we are all fragments of this same Primal Universal Creative Essence, *It seeks to express itself through each of us differently*. Thus we reflect the varied colours of the rainbow, so to speak, each of a hue slightly different from the rest, and so provide the fullest possible extent and scope for Its Creative Powers to express themselves in and through us during the evolutionary process.

Thus do we find, through the doctrine of *Swabhâva*, yet further enlightenment vouchsafed to us in the understanding of the meaning and purpose of human life, which it is the general aim of Theosophy to bring to Western man. Instead of regarding himself as a stranger in the Universe as heretofore (an alien with no real relationship with anything, either inside or outside himself), Western man can now know that within him he possesses a spark of divinity which links him directly with the Creative Source of All in the Universe, and which spark of divinity, in each individual case, has its own special and particular shade of colour in the universal kaleidoscope. This it is each person's destiny and duty to bring to its fullest and purest consummation as that particular shade or colour or aspect of Divine Creative Power working through him as man.

Once he has reached this stage of development, man feels himself not only akin to the Universe, but an essential part of it. Through striving to make himself more and more that part (in actuality instead of in potentiality, as hitherto), he co-operates consciously with the Universal Life Principle and becomes a co-worker with It. Thus he achieves a happiness and bliss impossible to men unaware of their true place in the Universal Scheme, drifting blindly along, impelled this way and that by their baser desires and impulses, seeking vainly for a happiness that can never be theirs, because sought for through the wrong motives and by the wrong means.

We all know that we share our common humanity with our fellowmen, but we also know that within us we each have qualities and aptitudes which distinguish us from our fellows, however limitedly this may be in some respects, and differing with different people. We do know, however, that we are *different*, and we feel that difference in our very bones, so to speak. That is what makes the doctrine of *Swabhâva* so important to us, personally. It gives us the reason for that feeling of difference we all possess. It shows us that through seeking to develop that difference which distinguishes us from our fellows we can make our fullest contribution to the life of humanity, generally, and at the same time play our part in furthering the evolutionary plan as devised by its Creative Mainspring or Source. We thus find that this doctrine brings hope and encouragement to even the most humble and lowly of men, for they realize that somewhere within them reside possibilities and potentialities for self-expression and creative effort which they alone are capable of, in their own particular way. And so they begin to feel that even they are worth something to the world, and are of value to the life of the whole.

Consider what this means to people continually frustrated by life and circumstance, and who believe that they are worthless both to themselves and to others. It gives new life and encouragement to them, and sets them upon the path of inner and upward development that can transform them into human beings of real worth and integrity, instead of remaining the mere flotsam and jetsam of society they are now.

Thus we find yet further proof of the profundity and value of the Theosophical teachings in the doctrine under discussion, and it shows the reader what a dynamic effect these teachings can have upon our lives once we accept and understand them, and begin to *really apply them*. Mere theoretical acceptance is worthless ; these teachings are meant to be applied in our own personal lives, otherwise they are quite valueless to us.

As we seek to put into practice these teachings in our lives, so we begin to see those lives becoming richer and fuller in every way, bringing real happiness in their train, and a contentment of spirit for which we sought before in vain. Of such worth are the fruits of Theosophy when given application in the lives of its students, and of such immense personal value are the teachings we have been dealing with in the brief survey of the present chapter.

CHAPTER VIII

THE DOCTRINE OF CYCLES; AND ROUNDS AND RACES

W E have brought the reader face to face with many startling and strange ideas and viewpoints during the course of the present book ; but in this chapter we venture to think we shall startle and puzzle him still further, in our attempts to describe the Doctrine of Cycles ; and Rounds and Races. It is not our wish to startle and puzzle the reader, but to increase his understanding of life and of himself. It does us good, however, to be jostled sometimes out of our usual intellectual complacency by having strange ideas and views thrust before us to upset our usual mode of thinking, and to provide us with a wider and deeper understanding of the Cosmos we inhabit.

H. P. Blavatsky used to talk about " breaking the moulds of mind " very often in her Theosophical writings, for she made it clear that only by so doing could further enlightenment enter the mind of the student. Without breaking the mould in which his mind had been set by current thought and customary thinking, it would be impossible to deepen his knowledge and understanding of the Universe and of himself. It would only be possible in that case to add to already existing trends of thought and thinking which had already greatly limited the student's ability to see into the secret workings of Universal Nature.

Thus, by startling and puzzling the reader we hope to " break the mould of his mind," and set his thought free for more aspiring journeys into the empyrean of truth and understanding. In no better way could we do this than by a discussion of the subject-matter of the present chapter. Here again, we are brought face to face with the vastness and profundity of the Theosophical teachings.

The *Doctrine of Cycles,* which it is our intention to discuss first in the present chapter, is also an age-old esoteric teaching, and refers to the fact that, despite its multifarious and enormously diversified aspects, the Universe is essentially simple in com-

THE DOCTRINE OF CYCLES

position and structure, and is made up of an infinite multitude of components, each with a certain definite *cycle of activity* of its own, of varying ranges of scope, significance and duration.

By the term " cycle of activity " we mean a definite schematic plan arranged thus: first a point of origin from which future activity begins; then a period of development of growth or function until a point of highest maturity or greatest attainment has been reached; then a gradual decline in power or growth leading to final cessation of physical function or manifestation, the whole process being cyclic (or *circular*) in plan or outline thus:

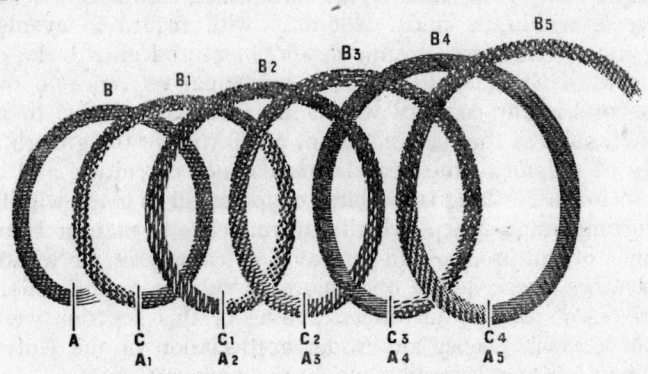

Points A and C do not quite coincide; if they did the Universe would remain completely static, just repeating itself over and over again endlessly as regards its outward forms or manifestations, without any inner onward growth or momentum of any kind. At point C a new cycle of activity (A1) begins, which will be related to the previous one as to time of origin and duration, by reference to the size or scope or function of the entity or object concerned, future cycles (or circles) of activity making with the first a sort of *infinite spiral* tracing-out the gradual evolution through time and space of the entity or object in question, as our diagram depicts.

The whole Universe is a vast network of such spirals of cycles of activity of lesser or greater degree; of " wheels within wheels," as it were, ranging in stature and status from the spiral of the cycle of life of a microbe, to that of a Cosmos, and embracing every shade and development of Universal Life. We are all aware of " the cycle of the seasons " ; of the cycle of day and night (of recurring light and dark) ; of the cycle of growth and decay of vegetable and animal life ; of the greater cycle of birth, maturity and death of the physical body of man. All these phenomena are various aspects of the *Doctrine of Cycles* to which we are referring.

Everything in the Universe has a cyclic basis according to the teaching just mentioned, we repeat, and that is why *Reincarnation* is so essentially a feature of Cosmic existence. It is, too, an expression of the same *Cyclic Law* which embraces the whole Universe within its folds. Not only with regard to events or happenings relating to cosmic development and growth does the Doctrine of Cycles hold good ; it has equal reference to every phase of life and activity within the Universe relative to man himself, such as the rise and fall of civilizations ; the growth and decay of religions ; the periodic renaissance of culture and art ; and so forth. Nothing is too large or too small to come within its all-encompassing sweep, whether of reference to man or Nature, thought or culture, cosmic upheaval or cataclysm, or whatnot. *Everything,* we reiterate once more, is subject to the action of Cyclic Law, and by an understanding of this doctrine we can obtain a much deeper and wider appreciation of the Universe and man's life and position within the Universe.

It is all too customary for mankind to assume that their own particular level of development is the highest yet attained by the human race. We realize immediately, however, what a mistake is such a view, once we begin to appreciate the all-embracing significance of the *Law of Cycles* just briefly outlined.

There have been epochs in man's chequered career on this globe when civilizations flourished which were far superior in every way to any known to recorded history, as regards culture, learning and refinement. But, in obedience to the operation of *Cyclic Law,* these civilizations have come and gone, had their day and vanished into the limbo of the past, in the vast majority of cases leaving behind them no visible traces of their existence.

It is not uncommon, however, for isolated clues to be picked up here and there by archaeologists of intelligence, and by anthropologists and geologists and others, which speak all too clearly

THE DOCTRINE OF CYCLES

of vanished races with cultures and arts that defy modern man's ability to approach and equal. Owing, however, to the ingrained belief in the mind of Western man that we have only been human beings on this earth for barely a few hundred thousand years (not long ago a few *tens* of thousands of years was the current belief), it is very hard for men working in the branches of science to which we have just referred to appraise their findings correctly. They tend to telescope all discoveries into epochs which are far shorter than is really the case, thus spoiling all chance of discovering the true state of affairs revealed by their findings, and thus making it very difficult to come upon a fair example of the operation of the doctrine we are discussing in the field in question.

Also, scientists in general are extremely loth to have it made public that civilizations existed in the past which put to shame our own. Such findings make it fairly obvious that our own civilization will likewise follow in the self-same path in due course, reaching its climax and apotheosis and in due time declining and disappearing. The modern mind cannot bear the thought of material annihilation for the civilization it is so proud of, because, not believing in any life after physical death for itself, it cannot willingly bring itself to accept death or final decay of present-day civilization, for in the latter it sees the only logical excuse for living! Besides, it abhors thinking of death or annihilation of any kind *in actuality*, however equably it may do so *in theory*!

Exactly as with civilizations and cultures of the past, so it is (or will be) with nations, empires, and cultures of the present or future. All these will have their rise, their climax of power and glory, then their gradual decay, giving place to other nations, empires and cultures (as witness the ancient glories of Egypt, Greece, and Rome, for example). This, too, is a most unwelcome thought for modern man to bear complacently, especially if he happens to belong to a nation which is a "great power." He likes to assume it will remain always a great power, even though evidence tells him that its grasp is slipping from the helm of world affairs, perhaps (as seems to be the case of the British Empire nowadays). "Wishful thinking" steps in, therefore, to blind the mind to what is actually taking place, in strict accordance with the operation of the universal principle here being dealt with. The same cyclic process is, of course, in progress with regard to the human body, too, in its rise to full growth, its maturity, and ultimate decay ; and so on and so forth, right throughout the whole of Cosmic Life, to the birth, rise to full glory, and decay of worlds and Universes.

What a vast sweep of inner cosmical working the Cyclic Doctrine reveals and makes clear to us, therefore. What a deepening of understanding and consciousness it gives, if we are ready to learn and accept what is thereby put before us. Our life-wisdom is enhanced enormously, because we can view all the phenomena of existence, from the very tiniest to the largest, through its gaze, so to speak. We are not bound by the moment ; we soar into the eternal, in our thought and comprehension!

Thus, then, does the *Doctrine of Cycles* open our eyes and vastly extend our vision, if we begin to appreciate its inner significance and apply it to universal life. We begin to have an entirely different outlook upon life, realizing that everything is in a state of flux, of becoming and departing, although within and through it all the Cosmic Life goes on ceaselessly without pause or end. Thus we gain a conception of immutable *Being* within *Becoming*, which is the real clue to Cosmic Existence. It also provides us with a proper perspective of our own time and age, and its place within the sweep of history.

It likewise provides us with a proper perspective of our own individual place within the general scheme of things, whether of to-day or of eternity. Surely a most refreshingly " mould-breaking " conception? It is a most welcome contrast to the static thought of the day, which always tries to keep its concepts and ideas within the bounds (and bonds) of neatly logical formulæ, killing all the dynamic sweep of life which should flow through them, and rendering them completely dead and lifeless as symbols which can explain the world we live in to the thoughtful and intuitive mind.

Modern thought, burdened by allegiance to logic and rationality, is a life-killing process, because it destroys the ebb and flow of the life-current working through phenomena, and substitutes static pieces of the lifeless exterior for exhibition, as it were. This is the main reason why all orthodox scientific thought is so unable to comprehend the real working of the Universe, and presents modern man with concepts which only puzzle his intuition and leave him the prey to ideas which are deadening and destroying to the spirit within.

When we turn to a conception such as the *Doctrine of Cycles*, therefore, we gain a picture of things which not only paves the way for deeper understanding, but gives the mind a mental fillip, sorely needed, by jerking it out of itself and setting into motion those deeper intuitional currents which modern man has effectively prevented from leavening his thought by his customary mode of thinking. So much, then, for the doctrine we have thus lightly touched upon. Its ramifications are immense, and have the power to unlock doors and mysteries undreamed of by the reader ; but we can say no more about the subject in the present book. If we have whetted the student's appetite for deeper study, that is sufficient for our present purpose.

Now let us turn to an even more startling and thought-provoking conception, which forms one of the principal Theosophical teachings ; that of the *Rounds and Races*. In some respects this is the most thought-shaking of all the Theosophical doctrines, and one which must make the student gasp with amazement that such mysteries should be unlocked before the eyes of modern Western man, who has so long prided himself on knowing " all the answers " and has regarded the thought and learning of the East as unworthy of consideration.

The doctrine of *Rounds and Races* comes from the ancient Eastern esoteric teachings, of course, like all the Theosophical Philosophy.

After even a cursory study of the doctrine, which is all that we can attempt in the present chapter, the reader should be feeling the humility of one who has been brought face to face with thoughts and ideas which touch the profoundest depths possible to the human intellect. Our modern age, though, with its customary mental conceit and superficiality of thinking, will no doubt regard them as merely so much fantastic nonsense, and forthwith dismiss them from its mind without further thought of any kind.

We have stressed repeatedly in the present book that everything connected with this Earth is septenary in character, the Earth itself having its own six finer bodies interpenetrating the dense physical mass which is all that we see ourselves of the globe we inhabit. But when we come to study the esoteric teaching of *Rounds and Races,* the first thing we learn is that not only is the Earth itself a septenary, but it requires *a series of seven Earths* (each following the other in turn as they appear on the cosmic scene) to make it possible for the scheme of evolution, of which humanity is a part, to complete its destined unfoldment during the present cycle of cosmic activity, under the impetus provided by the inherent Creative Force at work therein.

We learn from the teaching that our own Earth is the fourth in the series, three previous Earth-Globes having preceded our own in time, while there will be three others to follow ours, after the latter has fulfilled its destiny and duly sunk into the limbo of the past.

This mighty conception of a series of seven earth-globes, upon which evolution proceeds, over an immensity of time which beggars finite comprehension, is yet further complicated, however, in its full understanding, by the fact—which the teaching being discussed discloses—that not only does the evolutionary process take place on each of the seven physical Earths in turn, as they follow each other in serial progression through the ages, as the giant plan of evolution unfolds itself, *but on their finer bodies as well.* That is to say, the more rarified bodies which compose the inner fabric of each earth are also taking their part in the evolutionary drama, just as the dense physical globes they are associated with. Thus, there is a " Chain of Globes " (as it is termed in the Esoteric Philosophy) connected with each earth-globe, each globe of the chain acting for a period as the home of succeeding " life-waves " of evolving entities, as the evolutionary cycle proceeds on its destined course through each chain.

Each Chain of Globes is also a septenary, as are the series of seven earth-globes with which each chain is associated. It must always be remembered, however, that the more rarified globes which form each chain with the dense physical earth-globes of the series, are not separate and distinct globes in the same sense as the earth-globes themselves. They are the finer and more rarified bodies of the earth-globes, as just explained, interpenetrating each other and the dense physical mass of each earth-globe ; and that is a point where many students of these teachings go astray. The more rarified globes form a chain of globes with each dense earth-globe in the series, seven earth-globes each with their own chain of globes, and each chain a septenary, as just indicated. It is not, however, forty-nine distinct and separate globes upon which the evolutionary spectacle proceeds, but *only upon seven distinct and separate earth-globes separated in time and space, each such earth-globe having associated with it six more rarified globes pertaining to its own inner nature and structure*. We have to stress this point again, to try to make it as clear as possible, for as just said, many students of these teachings—many of them students of long standing and with much Theosophical learning—go wrong here.

We have already said in the chapter on Evolution that there are seven distinct groups of evolving entities associated with the human evolutionary process, ranging from the first elemental kingdom, through the second and third elemental kingdoms, the minerals, plants and animals, to man. And each of these seven "life waves" of evolving entities completes the round of each globe of each chain in the series, attaining gradually more and more towards full development along its particular evolutionary path as it progresses through each globe of each chain and through each series of chains.

The esoteric teaching associated with the conception in question is most involved, it must be confessed, and we can do no more than hint at the matter here. It must be left to the student to gain a more comprehensive understanding of the subject when he comes to study the more advanced Theosophical literature.

In passing, it must be noted that when each evolving "life-wave" has passed in turn through each of the seven globes of a chain, this is known as *one complete Round*. When this step in evolutionary development has been achieved, the earth-globe of that chain of globes begins to disintegrate, and finally dies out altogether, remaining for a time, however, as the moon of the succeeding earth-globe, our present moon being all that is left of the earth-globe of the third "Globe-Chain," while our own earth will in turn become the moon of the fifth earth-globe in the series.

When the seven complete rounds of the seven chains of globes have been completed, the evolutionary stream, of which our present humanity is the apex, will come to a pause for a time, prior to taking up its further evolutionary development on further series of globes outside our ken. The whole process of evolutionary procedure through each globe on each chain, and between chains, is punctuated by periods of cosmic repose, during which time all life sinks to the merest flicker, preparatory to starting up again with renewed vigour and vitality for a fresh start on the next globe or chain of globes of the series.

Likewise, when the full seven rounds of the whole series have been completed, there takes place a prolonged cessation of life-activity for a period commensurate with the time taken for the evolutionary process to have worked its way through the whole seven rounds, rest and activity balancing each other always in the work of cosmic creation (although the rest of repose is not death, just an in-drawing of forces for recuperation and replenishment, prior to further expression of the cosmic creative urge).

What a marvellous picture this presents of the work of cosmic creative activity; and how puny do the current evolutionary views of our day seem in comparison!

When the present writer first came into touch with these ideas, he felt that his mind was breaking loose from shackles which had held it prisoner for ages, as it were, and was at long last winging its way, free and untrammelled, into the world of true creative ideation, where the mind gains inspiration and courage and feels itself to be working in an entirely different medium from the thought-world of our day. The customary thought-patterns of our age and time are too puny for such vast conceptions. One has truly to "break the moulds of mind" to set free the inner aspiring consciousness to soar into the realms of creative intellection where one can grow mental limbs, as it were, and endeavour to follow, however humbly, in the footsteps of the mental giants of antiquity who were able to intuit and set down such vast cosmical concepts.

We would also like to make clear to the reader at this point, that, just as the earth we inhabit takes part in the vast scheme of evolution as here depicted, however feebly, by the writer, so must it be borne in mind that each Planet of our Solar System is likewise the centre of its own special system or type of evolution, quite distinct from our own, and with its own chains of globes and series of physical globes, exactly as with the Earth.

On each planet evolution is taking place, throughout the ages, in its own particular way and with its own special emphasis. Furthermore, on the Sun itself the identical process is proceeding likewise, with a series of suns following each other in time, in serial progression, and each sun with its chain of globes associated with it, evolution proceeding on each globe of each chain exactly as with the Earth, as just briefly described.

Of course, we are able to understand very little of the details of such further intricate permutations and combinations of the vast and complicated evolutionary panorama conjured up before the mind's eye ; such concepts make the mind boggle just to entertain the idea of them. But it is good for man to realize that his own particular scheme of evolution is only one in a vast and, indeed, infinite series of schemes of evolution taking place on every planet of every solar system in the Universe, and on the central suns of each such solar system too.

Thus does the mind broaden in outlook, and man become more humble in thought and deed, because he realizes that he is far from being the "king-pin" in the Universal Evolutionary Plan, as Darwinism had naïvely imputed. Man has to learn humility in the face of such vast and cosmical conceptions, and the more humble he can become, in the real sense, the more wisdom and true understanding will come his way. Then his mind and heart will be really open for inspiration and guidance, and the truth will surely flow in to him, in accordance with Cosmic Law.

Having given this necessarily brief and all-to-cursory sketch of the esoteric teaching referring to the *Rounds and Chains*, it is now time to say a few words regarding the conjoint teaching relative to the races of mankind, and their development during the evolutionary process. As usual in all occult matters relating to this Earth, *seven* is the key number involved. We learn that there are seven great "Root Races" of mankind, which make the round of each chain of globes associated with each of the seven earth-globes of our scheme of evolution, thereby gradually becoming more and more evolved types of humanity in the process.

In the very dim and distant past, when mankind was in the nascent stage, during the *First Round,* the seven root races were more a shadow than a reality, and man propagated himself by fission as protoplasmic cells do to this very day. Then, in the *Second Round,* man became hermaphrodite, having elements of both male and female organs within him, and thereby self-propagating his kind, the seven root races still being more nebulous than actual. It was only later, during the *Third Round,* that the sexes became separate and more or less as we know them to-day, and the seven root races became distinct entities.

These events all took place in earlier rounds, as just said, cosmical ages ago, we being at present in the *Fourth Round,* and our Earth being the fourth earth-globe in that round of the seven which will complete the series for that round. But these developments in man's history are recapitulated in a condensed form *in every round,* we are told, with certain variations peculiar to certain rounds and stages of evolution. We are given to understand that in the *Sixth Round* (and therefore in the *Sixth Root Race, too,* because there is a special recapitulative link between a root race and a round bearing the same number, according to the esoteric teaching), mankind will again be *bi-sexual,* propagation of the species no longer taking place as we know it to-day, this from the occult point of view being but a temporary phase in the cycle of human biological development. Incidentally, it is estimated in esoteric circles that the separation of the sexes in the present round, which took place during the *Third Root Race,* occurred 18,000,000 years ago!

Of the seven root races of our present globe we are the *Fifth,* the Third having been the *Lemurian,* the Fourth the *Atlantean,* and the present Fifth Root Race being the *Aryan.* In each root race there are seven Sub-Races, and each root race takes its name from the dominant sub-race in it, there always being one sub-race (corresponding in number to that of the root race in question) which dominates each particular root race, the third sub-race having been the dominant sub-race in the third root race; the fourth sub-race in the fourth root race; and the fifth sub-race in the fifth root race, and so on.

From the sixth sub-race that will follow our present Aryan fifth sub-race (which gives its name to the whole root race) will spring the germs of the *Sixth Root Race.* The third root race was called *Lemurian* having been domiciled on the lost continent

THE DOCTRINE OF CYCLES

of Lemuria ; and the fourth root race was *Atlantean,* having been domiciled on the lost continent of Atlantis. As each root race approaches its close, the Earth becomes convulsed, the old landmasses disappear, and an entirely different land-formation appears to house the newly developing root race which is to continue on it the human tradition. For further and fuller details regarding this fascinating and absorbing subject, the reader is again referred to the more advanced Theosophical literature. In that he will find the matter gone into in great detail, showing the wonderful exactness of the knowledge of the past held by the forerunners of the present custodians of the Ancient Wisdom.

We have said that our own special scheme of evolution was formerly on the " Moon Chain," and it is instructive to note that certain Planets of our Solar System are ahead of us in the type of evolution taking place on them, while others are behind us in evolutionary development.

For instance, the evolution taking place on Venus is greatly in advance of our own. Indeed, it was from Venus whence came those teachers of infant mankind who were those ordained in the Hierarchical Evolutionary Plan to help on its first uncertain steps in culture, refinement and art, and plant in its nascent mind and heart the seeds for future mental and spiritual development. In short, from Venus came all the mental, cultural and spiritual impetus that helped humanity to make its first civilizations possible. So that to the planet Venus humankind is eternally in debt, a karmic debt which can only be repaid by helping on other and less evolved evolutions on other planets when we are of sufficient spiritual and mental advancement to be able to do so.

The evolutions on Mars and Mercury are regarded as less evolved than our own. The idea held in some Theosophical circles that these two planets are associated with our own earth-chain of globes is quite erroneous, and arose from a misunderstanding on the part of Mr. A. P. Sinnett, one of the early expounders of the Theosophical Philosophy, and propagated in his books.

The reader can now see what a vast and immense gulf exists between the Theosophical conceptions regarding evolution and the development of man, and those of current scientific thought. The two attitudes are poles apart, and it is interesting to note how, as the years advance, further discoveries are made which confirm the Theosophical viewpoint in all kinds of unexpected and important ways.

As already said, the custodians of scientific thought always tend to disregard theories and discoveries which conflict with their own pre-conceived views, in spite of the fact that they are supposed to be always seeking for *the truth*. It will no doubt be centuries before the epoch-making Theosophical views and ideas (all taken from esoteric teachings of vast antiquity, be it noted) become acceptable to the " SCIENTIFIC " minds of the day. Before that can happen, the present supercilious attitude of Western man towards the thought and philosophy of the East will have had to undergo a radical transformation.

We hope that, in the present and preceding chapters, we have been able to present to the reader, however inadequately, some faint conception of the wonder and magnificence of the evolutionary spectacle taking place on our own planet and on the planets of our solar system, as well as on the sun itself. It is, indeed, breath-taking to feel for the first time, as do all new students of Theosophy, that they are part of a vast and intricate network of streams of evolution having their origin and development in every nook and cranny of the Universe, and intersecting and engulfing each other at all points, as it were, albeit to the majority of people quite unseen and unknown.

It makes one far more humble in thought and outlook to know that man is by no means the only type of key product being moulded in the ovens of the evolutionary furnace ; greater intellects by far are ahead of him, and greater thought and culture than he can ever aspire to have preceded his advent on the cosmic scene.

But, at least, it is something to know and feel that we are part and parcel of the gigantic " Evolutionary Whirligig " sweeping irresistibly onwards through the infinitudes of Space and Time, each of us linked by his inmost essence to the Central Cause of All, and expressing different facets of Its Creative Essence and Power through the various steps and stages of that evolutionary journey we have very inadequately attempted to portray in the present and preceding chapters. Surely, if anything can fire the aspiration and creative imagination of man, these concepts and ideas should!

CHAPTER IX

MAN'S DIVINE DESTINY; BROTHERHOOD A BASIC FACT IN NATURE

IF the foregoing pages have proved anything, it is surely that man is an integral part of the Universe and is linked indissolubly with it. His destiny, as man, has likewise been made clear for all to see ; a destiny which brings joy and comfort to all who can apprehend the full significance of that ultimate end of human sojourns and wanderings down the long vale of incarnate existence. That destiny is nothing less than *Godhead,* attained slowly and painfully through the ages by seeking for ever-better ways and means of giving expression to the God-like qualities and attributes man possesses by virtue of the fact of his divine source and parentage. Man's destiny is, indeed, a great and noble one. It lies in striving to show forth, in ever-increasing splendour, until the stage of *his own divinity* is reached, those regal powers and potentialities conferred on him by his " Father in Heaven," as a son of that " Father," a particle of whose Divine Essence he carries with him from the dawn of his days, and which particle is the source and basis of all that is best and finest in him.

To the average individual, the idea that man is a god in potential seems just sacrilege, as he has been brought up to believe that there is only one " God " who rules over the destinies of all with inscrutable will and in incomprehensible ways. Therefore, to speak in the same breath, as it were, of the divinity of man and his potential apotheosis as a *God in his own right* seems blasphemous to the average mind of to-day. But once we have absorbed the Theosophical teachings, as briefly set forth in the preceding pages, the fact stares us in the face. For, being a facet or particle of Divinity, and sharing in the life and creative powers of that Divinity, however limitedly, it stands to reason that as we progress up the evolutionary ladder, we are destined to show forth more and more of those qualities of divinity we possess. The time must inevitably arrive, therefore, when erstwhile man has at last become that which he was intended to be from the very beginning of time: *a God, with all the powers and attributes of Godhead.*

Obviously, such an end to man's career as man will take aeons of further existence to arrive at, needing much purgation of lower qualities and desires, and entailing much travail and suffering; but it is inevitable for all that, and naught can gainsay it. It is something that *must be,* however distant the day and time of its arrival.

We have mentioned previously " The Path " which the student of Occultism can traverse to shorten the evolutionary journey from man to that which lies beyond and higher than man. It is a path which provides a " short cut " through the tangled and wearisome evolutionary wanderings of incarnation after incarnation of the slowest possible spiritual progress and development, such as is the lot of the average type of human being, unaware of the god-like qualities he possesses, and the destiny in store for him. This path is common to all Esoteric Schools of Training (including the Mystery Schools of antiquity), and is the name given to that system of inner development whereby the neophyte is enabled to gain more and more control over his lower nature and give expression to the higher and more spiritual qualities he possesses. Thereby, in time, he is able to make progress in spirituality and spiritual attainment quite impossible to the individual following the slow pathway of ordinary human development with no idea at all as to his purpose and significance within " the all-embracing ' Scheme of Things'." The latter individual will arrive at his destined goal in due course, as we have stated, for it is a destiny which all *must* achieve. But, whereas it will mean aeons and aeons of time for the unthinking mass of mankind to arrive at this pre-ordained end of their human sojourn, the disciple on the Path will shorten the journey perhaps to a thousandth part, or even more.

As just said, the " Path of Discipleship " is common to all Schools of Esoteric Training, and its steps are portrayed most nobly and poetically in *The Voice of the Silence,* by H. P. Blavatsky. The " Noble Eightfold Path " of Buddhism points in the same direction. All effort and endeavour which directs itself towards seeking to bring into actuality those qualities of Love, Harmony, Sympathy, Restraint, Forbearance, Altruism, and other feelings, aspirations, and emotions of a like character, which all of us have in germ form within us, by virtue of our divine inheritance, and which especially characterize the one who is attempting to live the life of the "God in Man," leads inevitably in the direction of the opening-up of the individual concerned to those higher phases of spirituality and spiritual attainment of which the one who traverses The Path becomes peculiarly aware. In short, spiritual development and attainment can be achieved in no other way than through the conscious striving to make oneself more and more the channel for the dissemination of the qualities and characteristics above referred to. They are qualities and characteristics which show forth the stirrings of the "God Within," and which, as one pursues that path of inner attainment and development, take more and more control and command of the individual. Love and Harmony are of the very essence of Cosmic Life, because being basic elements in that Divinity which encompasses all within Its Mighty Folds. All endeavour to bring out those qualities in ourselves and radiate them throughout our daily tasks and activities inevitably brings us closer to the "God in Man," and to the Divine Source of all such Godhead.

Here, again, it is only the working out of Cosmic Laws which are an integral feature of all existence, and which laws were already fully known to the founders of the Esoteric Philosophy at its inception in times immemorial. The one who would traverse The Path will find the way hard and stony, and beset with all sorts of snares and pitfalls, not the least being his own desire for spiritual development.

For, if we desire spiritual development for its ability to confer on us powers and special aptitudes which we covet, then we are setting a barrier to such spiritual development which nothing can overcome. We shall fail in our aspiration and endeavour, simply because our desire has been tinged with personal longing and personal conceit, however much it may have been disguised by its spiritual character.

Only to the one who seeks such development for the power and ability it confers on him *to help his fellow-men more fully,* and for no personal reasons of any kind, will his efforts bring forth their destined fruits, and more and more spirituality and spiritual attainment be forthcoming. For altruism is the keynote of all spiritual achievement along The Path, and truly one can say here: " Not for myself but for Mankind do I make my endeavours."

Only by one's steadfast desire to help suffering humankind can one be aided in one's strivings to travel The Path, because only so can the strength to overcome the difficulties of the journey be arrived at. It is not for the puny in spirit, nor even for those of strength of character but seeking their own personal spiritual ends ; it is only for the " pure in heart " who seek such spiritual development simply for the power it confers on them for helping others less fortunate or less evolved in their evolutionary strivings.

In dealing, however briefly, with the question of man's divine destiny and the steps whereby this innate divinity can be realized and brought into actuality—however uncertain this may be of achievement at our present level of evolutionary development— there are two most important facts that need stressing. The first is that, from the esoteric point of view, everything that goes to make up the world within which we live (the objects that surround us, the impressions we obtain through our senses, the whole *milieu* of our existence, as it were), is merely *Mâyâ* (or *illusion*). This is not to say the world does not exist, it certainly has existence in so far as it is cognizable through our senses, thoughts and feelings ; but it is merely the outward covering, as it were, of the inner spiritual essence of things, which is the only *abiding reality*. *Mâyâ* is a Sanskrit word, and many people have assumed that it meant that the world we inhabit and the things of sense, generally, are completely illusory and mere figments of the imagination ; but this is quite wrong. As just pointed out, the world of sense certainly exists, and we have to live in it for the purposes of our inner spiritual development. It is, however, only the outward impermanent husk or rind of reality. The only things that have such reality and are such reality are the spiritual verities which clothe themselves in such outward trappings— trappings that are all too subject to decomposition and decay.

Spirit must needs clothe itself in matter to make itself actual to beings with such limited powers and potentialities as ourselves. The meaning of *Mâyâ* is essentially the illusory (in the sense of *temporar*) characteristic or quality of external Nature and external happenings and events, generally, as compared with the inner spiritual reality which endures *for all time*. The inner is always the real, the actual; the outer, the external, is always that which is destined to disappear, to decay and disintegrate, after the inner spiritual reality which has used it as its vehicle has discarded it as being of no further use or value.

If we always bear this fact in mind it will save us a very great deal of trouble, for people tend to pin their attention and even their faith on the external happenings of life, and tend to ignore entirely the inner spiritual forces which make use of, and express themselves through, those external events and happenings. Thus, if one fixes one's gaze exclusively on this external " shadow-show " which is destined to decay and disappear sooner or later, in accordance with Cosmic Law, one is sure to be disappointed and misled. Whereas, if one ignores the " outward seeming " and its appeal to eye and brain and ear, and concentrates upon the *spirit within* the particular event or happening, one is then *rooted in reality and in eternity*, in thought, conduct, and aspiration, and so can never be disappointed or led astray in the hurly-burly of life. That is the essential significance of the esoteric teaching regarding the world of *Mâyâ*, and, as we hope the reader now understands, it is a significance of the most profound value to man's spiritual development.

The second fact we would like to stress, in connection with the subject-matter of the present chapter, is that, in striving to live the spiritual life, many are led into the error of assuming that physical life and the events and affairs of every-day existence are of very little consequence in the course of such striving. Never was there a greater mistake, however, and many indeed are they who have wrecked their spiritual careers by such mistaken belief and action.

It is most important indeed to realize that although the spiritual life is the only life that really matters to the aspiring soul of man, we all have to live our lives in and through the physical body and on this physical Earth. To neglect or attempt to ignore the physical, therefore, and concentrate all our attention and endeavour on things spiritual is really defeating our own ends.

Fortunate are they who realize this vitally important fact, for it can save them from making a complete wreck of their lives, once their eyes have been opened to the need for spiritual striving and the desire for such striving has been borne in on their consciousness. It is at that point the danger arises of imagining that physical things and physical events are not worth bothering about, being on a plane beneath that on which we are henceforth seeking to live our lives. The fact is, as above intimated, we can only live in and through our physical bodies in our present stage of human development, and everything has to be performed on this physical globe.

It is a point well worth noting by people in danger of committing the mistake just referred to *that it is only on this physical plane that the bad Karma of the past can be adjusted satisfactorily, and the proper steps taken to ensure that we do not pile up future bad Karma to entrap us in later lives on Earth*. In other words, it is on the physical plane and in the physical world that we make or unmake Karma. In and on all other planes, no matter how exalted, we can only deal with *the consequences* of karmic action set on foot by what we do or do not do in our physical-plane lives. Surely a thought of the profoundest significance to those who would live the life of the spirit? As with the other subjects raised and dealt with in preceding chapters we feel that this is as far as we can go with the particular matter in hand in a book which sets out to give the reader only a cursory glimpse of the wonder and magnificence of the Theosophical teachings, and whet his appetite for deeper study. We must, therefore, leave the student to turn to the more advanced Theosophical literature for further consideration of the all-important matters affecting the life and destiny of man.

We now wish to turn to a subject which is closely allied to what we have just been discussing, and say a few words about that before bringing the present chapter to a close. We refer to that part of the chapter-heading which reads: *Brotherhood as a Basic Fact in Nature*. We have said previously that Love and Harmony are basic realities in Universal Life, proceeding from the nature of the *Primal Causeless Cause of All*, so that the more these qualities can be built up in our own natures and disseminated far and wide throughout the world, the better will be the prospects of that amity and concord between men which all thoughtful and discerning people wish to see. The possibility of such amity and concord in a world racked by oft-recurring wars of increasing destructiveness and range, seems rather far off, unfortunately, but, for all that, it is an ideal which *must* be striven for by those seeking to live the life of the spirit ; for to give up hope would be fatal. Even though the outlook be gloomy in the extreme, and the prospects most discouraging, it is, nevertheless, the duty of all those wishing to foster the spirit of true accord among men to seek to disseminate the qualities of Love and Harmony through their thought and conduct, and in all activities which bring them into contact with their fellow-men. Thus they may strive to set up a gradually increasing barrier against the almost overwhelming tides of Hatred and Discord which now seem to hold most men in their thrall.

It is usual to think of "Love" as sentimental affection for others, but this is completely erroneous. By love we mean a realization of the essential spiritual kinship existent between all men by virtue of their common divine origin and destiny, and an attempt to express that feeling of spiritual unity and accord in all affairs affecting our relationships with others.

This fact of our common divine origin and destiny makes *Brotherhood* (*real spiritual brotherhood*) an integral factor in human life ; and, indeed, shows it to be one of the basic laws of Nature, once we begin to reason correctly about the matter. There have been many men (especially in recent times) who have been imbued with a desire to help their fellows, and who have spoken about the "Brotherhood of Man." They have striven through the medium of social and political changes to bring better conditions of life and living to their fellows ; but that kind of brotherhood is not at all what we mean. The latter is based on the realization of the kinship which exists between men by virtue of their common needs and social and political aspirations ; and it is not that *brotherhood of the spirit* to which we are referring. The two conceptions are poles apart, although superficially they may appear very much like each other. It is only when one realizes the great gulf that exists between these two ways of looking at the subject of brotherhood that the full implications of the esoteric viewpoint become clear to us. It is easy enough to say we regard all men as brothers, if what we mean by that is simply that they are joint heirs to the wealth and comfort that civilization can provide, and deserve each their full share in such " good things of life."

It is far harder, however, to try to really feel one's spiritual kinship with all one's fellow-men and strive to bring out more and more fully the qualities of Love and Harmony in all our relationships with them, in order to prove by deed and not merely by word that we truly feel that *brotherhood of the spirit* with all that it implies. In the first case it is merely a mental recognition of fellowship between men ; in the second case it is a bond of spiritual kinship felt in the heart and nourished there constantly by proper thought, feeling and conduct towards mankind, and, indeed, towards the animal kingdom and sentient life generally, all being part of the same universal process of evolutionary development of spirit through matter.

One of the basic tenets of Theosophy is this acceptance of the fact of the *Brotherhood of Man* (in the sense we have endeavoured to ascribe to it in these pages) ; and, indeed, for those wishing to join the Theosophical Society it is the only one of its aims that must receive the whole-hearted support of the entrant. All other aims and objects can be disregarded by the one wishing to join, should he so desire ; but the *Brotherhood of Man* (in the sense here depicted, and as a basic fact and law in Nature), *must be* accepted by all. Without that cement to weld together the inner spiritual fabric of the entrant into the *Theosophical Way of Life*, he or she could never start out on the spiritual journey with any hope of success. The essence of Theosophy is to acquire self-knowledge to enable us to HELP OUR FELLOWS. Without the realization of what that *really* means, in terms of spiritual brotherhood, the outcome must necessarily be failure, sooner or later, no matter how much " brain-knowledge " may be acquired during the course of one's studies (which brings us on directly to the subject-matter of the next and final chapter).

CHAPTER X

THEOSOPHY AS A WAY OF LIFE AS WELL AS A PHILOSOPHY OF LIVING; PITFALLS ON THE PATH OF OCCULTISM

IT is our sincere hope that in reading through the preceding chapters the newcomer to Theosophy has found therein the answer to the vexed problems of life and living he or she has been seeking. In no more suitable manner could the writer be repaid for whatever effort and labour have been entailed in producing this volume than to know that it has been instrumental in bringing to others the priceless boon of Theosophy which he himself was accorded some years ago.

The first thing one feels, when coming into touch with the reality of the Theosophical teachings, is the desire to pass on the knowledge to others. One feels *impelled* to do so ; and, indeed, to do so is incumbent upon all Theosophists, once they have joined the Movement. From no man or woman capable of understanding something at least of the Theosophical conception of life, and eager to learn of it, must the knowledge be kept back ; it is intended for all, and *must* be for all, in accordance with their ability to take from it and learn from it.

But many who have come into touch with Theosophy, while appreciating the significance of it as a philosophy of living (i.e., its ability to clarify their minds in respect of the many and perplexing problems which formerly have beset them, with regard to an understanding of the Universe and its mysterious workings, and man's place therein), seem to believe its usefulness ends there, very much as with the academic philosophies of the Schools and Universities. *Never was there a greater mistake!* If Theosophy was merely something for study, something to act as a sort of mental gymnastics to exercise one's brains, it would be a sheer waste of time and effort for people to dedicate their lives to its propaganda throughout the world, as so many have done.

No, indeed; Theosophy is a *way of life* as well as a philosophy of living, and that is where its unique value comes in. It not only shows man what is the meaning and purpose of existence, and his own special significance within the Universal Whole, it also shows him *how to live his life* to the best and fullest within his power, and so make himself a *conscious co-worker with Nature* in pursuance of the ends inherent within the Great Cosmical Plan, as revealed to him by his study of the Theosophical teachings.

From the time of man's first appearance on Earth, long before the dawn of recorded history, Great Beings have existed whose purpose it was to show man the "why and wherefore" of his existence, and indicate the means whereby he might make himself an intelligent partner and co-operator in the working of that vast Cosmical Evolutionary Scheme revealed to him by these selfsame Great Beings, thereby fulfilling his destiny *as man*, and helping on the evolution of sentient life generally.

Down the ages Great Teachers have come forward from time to time to carry on the ancient tradition, pointing the way again and again to erring mankind, whenever the need was greatest. Their teachings have become enshrined in world religions and philosophies which, however much they may have become distorted and perverted through misunderstanding of their true significance, have helped nevertheless many millions to make themselves far better and more worth-while beings than would otherwise have been the case.

It is a fundamental tenet of the Theosophical Philosophy that all the Great Teachers come from the same "Great Lodge of Adepts" who watch over the destiny of our Globe, teaching always *the same doctrines* for those with the necessary ears to hear (however different the style and manner of their utterances might be), and shielding always their more esoteric pronouncements from the ears of the unthinking multitude by speaking in allegory or parable (as did the Great Gautama the Buddha, and Jesus the Christ, for instance).

All such Great Teachers have passed on the *same message*, we repeat, however varied its form of presentation, and all the great religions and philosophies of the past bear witness to the truth of this statement when examined with the inner seeing eye, i.e., according to the spirit rather than the letter.

It is this traditional body of truth, handed down the ages for the teaching and edification of mankind (or rather that portion of it capable of thinking for themselves), which has been collected together and presented to the Western World under the present-day guise of Theosophy. The reader can therefore appreciate the truly onerous responsibility which such knowledge entails on those who have studied the Theosophical teachings and had their whole outlook on life entirely changed thereby. It is incumbent on all such people to strive to show forth in their daily conduct their appreciation of what the truths they have imbibed *have really meant to them* (i.e., in their attitude to the daily problems of life which beset them ; in their attitude to their fellow men and women ; in the manner in which they meet adversity and suffering ; in short, in the whole conduct and mode of their living). *Only in such manner can they show clearly that they have understood what they have been learning, and that they have profited thereby.*

Let us emphasize, again, Theosophy is essentially a *way of life* as well as a philosophy of living, and we can only comprehend the inner reality of the latter aspect of it by constantly striving to put into practice what we have absorbed of its teachings in our daily mode of life. Otherwise the whole thing becomes a mere sham and hollow mockery, and no good whatsoever can result. In other words, Theosophy is essentially for those who have the courage to attempt to live the *Theosophical Life,* thereby helping on their fellows in evolutionary development by precept and example, without perhaps saying a word to anyone about their Theosophical studies.

Precept and example act upon the mind and consciousness of others in a most penetrating way, whereas mere " windy utterances " do not, however much they may seem to do so superficially. In short, it is deeds rather than words that count here, as with so much else in life ; although the student of Theosophy must be always ready to expound the Theosophical teachings—as far as lies within his power—to all those intimating their desire to hear about them. There is no denying, however, that to be able to expound Theosophy to all manner and types of individuals is no mean ability; indeed, it is beyond the power of many earnest Theosophists, requiring, as it does, exceptional intellectual ability combined with great clarity of verbal expression. If one has not the intellectual requirements for such a task, there is no need to feel downcast. *Trying to live one's Theosophy* can often do more and bring in more new adherents than mere ability to expound the teachings.

In a world which does not know where to turn for guidance and counsel—a world which has no touchstone which can detect right from wrong and all too often substitutes expediency for truth in its dealings—in a world such as this, it is indeed a great thing to be able to have a sure and firm knowledge of the way in which one's life should be lived, and be able to pass on that assurance in one's contacts with one's fellows. It acts as a beacon of light, as it were, in a world of shadows, whereby many who have lost the way or see its outline but dimly, can trace out anew its well-worn flagstones, treading forward again with firmness and courage, assured at last that they will be led straight into a realm where the basic verities *Truth, Goodness and Beauty* reside, ready to reveal themselves more and more to our inward gaze as we seek to put into practice the ethical principles inherent within the Theosophical Philosophy.

It is quite possible to delude oneself (and possibly others) that one is leading the *Theosophical Life* when one is seeking merely to show off one's spiritual gifts and attainments. The way is beset with many pitfalls and difficulties, it must be admitted, for even in such matters (and perhaps even more so here than elsewhere, because of what is at stake) the lower nature (or *personality*) is for ever striving to gain ascendancy over the inner self (or *individuality*), and will exploit any avenue open to it, even the most spiritual. So that it behoves all those who wish to make Theosophy the touchstone of their lives, and walk in its light, to be for ever on their guard against their lower nature and the many and various stratagems to which it will resort to defeat the ends set before it by the inner aspiring soul. But that is the very thing with which "The Path" we have already spoken about is concerned, so that the reader can now see that the very fabric of spiritual development and attainment is bound up with the living of what we have here called the *Theosophical Life*.

Such a mode of life confers blessings on all who come into contact with the one living it, through the inspiring and uplifting radiations he is for ever putting forth into the surrounding atmosphere. These radiations impinge inevitably on other men and women in their passing and stimulate in them like qualities, albeit all unknown to them. Thus one does good work by stealth, once one has dedicated one's life to its propagation among men.

Far be it from the writer to have the reader believe, however, that he or other Theosophists of his acquaintance (with the possible exception of a solitary one here and there) measure up fully to all the Theosophical requirements in the mode and conduct of their life. We but strive to put into practice, however feebly, such precepts and principles, and the rest must be left to time to show forth what will be the results. It would be folly for the interested reader, therefore, to become afraid of taking up Theosophy or joining the Movement for fear of being deemed " unworthy." We are all equally unworthy, and at the same time all equally worthy. Given the incentive to do our best *to help our fellows* and strive to make the utmost of our lives with the light that Theosophy has brought to us, all else is forgiven. Thus, there need be no diffidence in coming forward as prospective members of the Movement once the newcomer feels that in Theosophy he or she has found what they have long been seeking.

The reader may well be pardoned for interjecting at this juncture the pertinent question: " This is all very well, but *does the Theosophical Life work*?" In other words: " Is it a life that one can lead in the world of to-day, with positive results to the one living in such wise?" To which we unhesitatingly reply: "*Yes, it does work!* It works in the sense that we gain a contentment of mind and spirit impossible to those living the ordinary type of life of to-day, with its pursuit of money, sensationalism, and a ' good time ' generally." It is a way of life that does not bring worldly success, obviously ; but it brings something far more worth-while than that—*real happiness in living*. That is something no wealth can buy, no matter how great! Moreover, it helps *others* as well as ourselves. Surely no mean achievement for a *way of life*?

At the same time, when viewing the type of life in question, there are certain dangers to be regarded, which might be called (as in our chapter-heading) *pitfalls on the path of Occultism*. Those dangers need stressing, and so upon a warning note about them we intend to draw the present book to its close.

In the first place the word *Occultism* has been given a rather sinister significance in many quarters, because it is associated and confused with occult practices such as psychism, magic, clairvoyance, and the like. But *Occultism* in its true sense means merely trying to live the *Theosophical Life* as here depicted; that and nothing more. The word *occult* has reference to hidden knowledge, and Theosophy is essentially the revelation of hidden knowledge of the ages to modern Western man.

So that the *Path of Occultism* is the *Theosophical Way of Life* in the true conception of that term. Occult practices, so-called, such as we have referred to, have no part in such a way of life, although, during the course of occult (i.e., spiritual) development one becomes the possessor of powers which may appear strange and magical to the average individual.

It is in attempting to tread the *Occult Path* merely for the purpose of attaining such occult powers that lies the chief dangers to the aspirant after spiritual development, and which constitutes the greatest stumbling-block of all to the individual concerned. Theosophical literature is full of warnings against such mistaken endeavour, for its consequences can be serious.

Then, again, there are those who are drawn into touch with Theosophy and Occultism merely by virtue of their rather morbid interest in things psychic and "miraculous," seeking always for new sensations in these directions, and unfortunately having their desires gratified often by some who set themselves up as teachers of Theosophy. Here, once more, is a great stumbling-block in the path of those seeking true Occult enlightenment. It therefore behoves all interested in the subject to tread warily and keep before them all the time the knowledge that *altruism* and a *desire* to help one''s fellows are the chief hall-marks of the genuine Theosophical Teacher, and not mere exhibition of occult powers or offers to teach others such powers.

Again, it is a fundamental axiom of true Theosophy that no money be made by its dissemination. Those who offer to teach any branch of Occultism for fees should be regarded by the person approached or interested with the greatest suspicion, therefore, for such individuals are suspect from the very start. They should be given as wide a berth as possible.

The true occult teaching is ready for all true seekers when they are at a stage to profit by it. It must assuredly come their way by virtue of the " inner call " sent out by the genuine seeker after enlightenment. Truly has it been said: " Seek and ye shall find ; knock and it shall be opened unto you " ; for every honest aspirant after occult truth will be drawn inevitably towards that which he is seeking. It is a Cosmic Law which cannot be gainsaid.

Yet, again, there are many who will seek to deride Theosophy, should the reader show that he or she is becoming interested in the subject, and attempt to interpose all sorts of obstacles in the way of further study ; so that there are many and often most sinister obstructions and difficulties in the path of those wishing to come in touch with occult teachings. But, if one has at heart the betterment of his fellows and holds fast within himself to the truth when once his inner intuition has apprised him of its existence (through having come into touch with some of the Theosophical teachings in one way or another), then nothing can draw him aside from the course he is henceforth destined to tread. His whole being will know with unshakable faith that what he is learning is, indeed, THE TRUTH ; and as he proceeds with his studies, so that *truth* will reveal itself ever more fully and clearly to the inner discerning eye.

Here, then, we venture to take leave of the reader, convinced that if he will but follow the inner conviction which the perusal of the foregoing pages should have built up within him, he will never regret the step taken in associating himself with the Theosophical teachings and the Theosophical Movement. He will henceforth become a focus as he radiates the spirit of his inner conviction amongst the people with whom he comes into contact, thereby leading more and more aspiring souls into touch with the epoch-making truths and teachings of Theosophy. Those truths and teachings which can change men overnight, as it were, if they are ripe for such knowledge, as assuredly they will be if brought into touch with it from motives of true desire for inner illumination in a world of black shadows, and fostered by a belief in their fellows and the goodness hidden away deep within the heart of even the most unpromising specimen of them.

THE END